Building a Web Application with PHP and MariaDB: A Reference Guide

Build fast, secure, and interactive web applications using this comprehensive guide

Sai Srinivas Sriparasa

[PACKT]
PUBLISHING

open source*
community experience distilled

BIRMINGHAM - MUMBAI

Building a Web Application with PHP and MariaDB: A Reference Guide

First published: June 2014

Production Reference: 1090614

Published by Packt Publishing Ltd.
Livery Place
35 Livery Street
Birmingham B3 2PB, UK.

ISBN 978-1-78398-162-5

www.packtpub.com

Cover Image by Artie Ng (artherng@yahoo.com.au)

Credits

Author
Sai Srinivas Sriparasa

Reviewers
Dario Grd

Nikolai Lifanov

Esteban De La Fuente Rubio

Commissioning Editor
Kunal Parikh

Acquisition Editor
Mohammad Rizvi

Content Development Editor
Shaon Basu

Technical Editors
Mrunmayee Patil

Aman Preet Singh

Copy Editors
Janbal Dharmaraj

Sayanee Mukherjee

Project Coordinator
Sageer Parkar

Proofreaders
Simran Bhogal

Stephen Copestake

Indexers
Hemangini Bari

Mariammal Chettiyar

Mehreen Deshmukh

Tejal Soni

Production Coordinator
Nitesh Thakur

Cover Work
Nitesh Thakur

About the Author

Sai Srinivas Sriparasa is a web developer and an open-source evangelist living in the Atlanta area. He was the lead developer for building Dr. Oz's website and currently works on predictive analysis algorithms for News Distribution Network (NDN). He has previously led teams for companies such as Sprint Nextel, West Interactive, Apple, and SAC Capital. His repertoire includes PHP, Python, MySQL, MariaDB, MongoDB, Hadoop, JavaScript, HTML5, Responsive Web Development, ASP.NET, C#, Silverlight, and so on. He has worked on books such as *JavaScript and JSON Essentials*, *Packt Publishing*.

I want to convey my sincere thanks to the team at Packt Publishing for making this book possible: Shaon, Sageer, and Sumeet in particular. This is my second book, so I want to thank all of the readers in advance for taking time to read my book. Please contact me on my LinkedIn profile, `http://www.linkedin.com/in/saisriparasa`, for networking or any questions that you have.

My acknowledgement section will not be complete unless I thank my mom, dad, and my sister for all their patience and support throughout my life. I hope you all enjoy this book as much as I did and wish me luck for my next book.

About the Reviewers

Dario Grd is a web developer with 7 years of experience in various technologies. He works with programming languages such as PHP, Java, Groovy, and .NET. He loves working with frameworks such as Symfony, Grails, jQuery, and Bootstrap.

He finished his master's degree in Informatics at the Faculty of Organization and Informatics, University of Zagreb. After getting the degree, he started working as a programmer at a company specialized in developing banking information systems, where he became a web team leader. Currently, he is working at the Faculty of Organization and Informatics as an expert assistant in Higher Education and Science System at Application Development Centre.

He works on various European and freelance projects. He developed a new Content Management System (CMS) from scratch and is very proud of it. Other than programming, he is also interested in web server administration and is currently managing a hosting server. When he is not working, you can find him on the soccer field or playing table tennis. He plays futsal for a local team and competes in an amateur table tennis league. You can follow him at
`http://dario-grd.iz.hr/en`.

Nikolai Lifanov hacks systems. This means doing things that aren't meant to be done to create a useful effect in a hurry. Over the last decade, he has had experience in everything from running HA infrastructures on donated prefail hardware to dealing with emergency spikes in service demand by padding the infrastructure with cloud services within hours. He had roles ranging from that of a full-stack engineer to a developer, but feels most in his element focusing on essential system infrastructure. He builds robust and observable systems that are hard to break and easy to fix with a strong focus on self-healing, security, and reducing essential ongoing maintenance. He has built solutions from Linux and BSD systems, from creating immutable live cd NetBSD hypervisors (a la SmartOS) to founding a hosting business based on DragonFly. He tries to be active in the open source community and enjoys old-school roguelike games. His hobbies include researching obscure ancient arcane Unix lore and retro computing.

Esteban De La Fuente Rubio is a programmer with experience mainly in the PHP language. He worked in his earlier years developing small websites and by now, 10 years later, he is the author of the *SowerPHP* framework on GitHub. In the last 6 years, he has worked for various Chilean companies developing software for supporting their process. He also contributed to the free software community developing small applications and tools to make life easier (more details on this can be found at his GitHub account, namely, `https://github.com/estebandelaf`).

www.PacktPub.com

Support files, eBooks, discount offers, and more

You might want to visit www.PacktPub.com for support files and downloads related to your book.

Did you know that Packt offers eBook versions of every book published, with PDF and ePub files available? You can upgrade to the eBook version at www.PacktPub.com and as a print book customer, you are entitled to a discount on the eBook copy. Get in touch with us at service@packtpub.com for more details.

At www.PacktPub.com, you can also read a collection of free technical articles, sign up for a range of free newsletters and receive exclusive discounts and offers on Packt books and eBooks.

http://PacktLib.PacktPub.com

Do you need instant solutions to your IT questions? PacktLib is Packt's online digital book library. Here, you can access, read and search across Packt's entire library of books.

Why subscribe?
- Fully searchable across every book published by Packt
- Copy and paste, print and bookmark content
- On demand and accessible via web browser

Free access for Packt account holders

If you have an account with Packt at www.PacktPub.com, you can use this to access PacktLib today and view nine entirely free books. Simply use your login credentials for immediate access.

Table of Contents

Preface

In the age of the Internet, building a web application is no longer a tough task, but building the web application in the right way is not a trait mastered by many. *Building a Web Application with PHP and MariaDB: A Reference Guide* is aimed at taking readers to the next level and to transform them from beginner-level programmers to intermediate or advanced-level programmers. *Building a Web Application with PHP and MariaDB: A Reference Guide* is a well thought out guide that begins with the basics of PHP and MariaDB and covers complex topics such as caching, security, building a REST API, and performance optimization. Building a web application that will be secure, scale well under pressure, and have an API available to different subscribers is not a simple task, but this book will make this a simple, easy-to-learn, and a memorable journey.

What this book covers

Chapter 1, CRUD Operations, Sorting, Filtering, and Joins, deals with introducing readers to basic SQL operations such as create, read, update, and delete. We then go to the next step by discussing sorting, filtering, and end by discussing the concept of joining tables.

Chapter 2, Advanced Programming with MariaDB, deals with various data manipulation operations such as alter and drop. After a clear understanding of the DML operations, we will discuss the more advanced concepts such as stored procedures, stored routines, and triggers.

Chapter 3, Advanced Programming with PHP, introduces readers to more advanced programming concepts such as unit testing and exception handling. We also discuss the new features that have been added to PHP 5.4 and 5.5.

Chapter 4, Setting Up Student Portal, deals with using all the concepts encompassed in the last few chapters to build a student portal.

Chapter 5, Working with Files and Directories, deals with the introduction and implementation of file imports, file uploads, and application logging using files in our student portal application.

Chapter 6, Authentication and Access Control, deals with the introduction and implementation of authentication and access controls for our student portal application.

Chapter 7, Caching, introduces the readers to the concept of caching. We later discuss the different types of caching and how each method of caching is implemented.

Chapter 8, REST API, introduces readers to the concept of REST architecture, followed by building a REST API for our student portal.

Chapter 9, Security, deals with an introduction to the different security optimizations that can be performed for Apache, MariaDB, and PHP to secure the web application.

Chapter 10, Performance Optimization, deals with the introduction of different performance optimization techniques that can be used to scale the application more effectively.

Bonus chapter 1, Installation of PHP, MariaDB, and Apache, deals with the installation and configuration of PHP, MariaDB, and Apache. This chapter is not present in the book but is available for download at `https://www.packtpub.com/sites/default/files/downloads/Bonus_chapter_1.pdf`.

Bonus chapter 2, Object-oriented Programming with PHP, deals with introducing the readers to the concept of Object Oriented Programming (OOP) with PHP and we continue by discussing various OOP features such as inheritance, encapsulation, polymorphism, interfaces, and abstract classes. We end this chapter by discussing a few popular design patterns. This chapter is not present in the book but is available for download at `https://www.packtpub.com/sites/default/files/downloads/Bonus_chapter_2.pdf`.

What you need for this book

This book deals with building web applications; so, to successfully host a web application, you will need the Apache web server. Once the request is received by the web server, it will forward that request to the server-side program, and we will be using PHP for our server-side scripting. We will be using MariaDB as our database server to store our data. We are using Memcache for memory caching. The software needed are: PHP, MariaDB, Apache server, cURL, and Memcache.

Who this book is for

This book has been designed to cater to the needs of developers at all levels. This book contains numerous examples, tips, and recommendations that will guide the readers from the installation and configuration phase to deployment phase. Prior knowledge of PHP, MariaDB, and/or Apache web server will be very helpful, but not required.

Conventions

In this book, you will find a number of styles of text that distinguish between different kinds of information. Here are some examples of these styles, and an explanation of their meaning.

Code words in text, database table names, folder names, filenames, file extensions, pathnames, dummy URLs, user input, and Twitter handles are shown as follows: "Upon executing the show databases; command, the list of existing databases will be outputted to the screen"

A block of code is set as follows:

```php
<?php
/**
* Array declaration before PHP 5.4
*
*/
$arr = array(1,2,3,4);
//Print an element to the screen
echo $arr[0];
/**
* Array declaration with PHP 5.4 or greater
*
*/
$arr2 = [1,2,3,4];
//Print an element to the screen
echo $arr2[0];
?>
```

Any command-line input or output is written as follows:

phpunit --version

New terms and **important words** are shown in bold. Words that you see on the screen, in menus or dialog boxes for example, appear in the text like this: "Now that the database has been successfully changed, note that the database name reflects in between the brackets next to **MariaDB**, which denotes the current database."

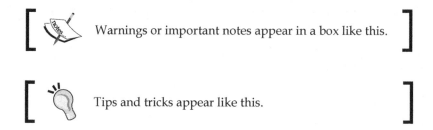

> Warnings or important notes appear in a box like this.

> Tips and tricks appear like this.

Reader feedback

Feedback from our readers is always welcome. Let us know what you think about this book—what you liked or may have disliked. Reader feedback is important for us to develop titles that you really get the most out of.

To send us general feedback, simply send an e-mail to feedback@packtpub.com, and mention the book title via the subject of your message.

If there is a topic that you have expertise in and you are interested in either writing or contributing to a book, see our author guide on www.packtpub.com/authors.

Customer support

Now that you are the proud owner of a Packt book, we have a number of things to help you to get the most from your purchase.

Downloading the example code

You can download the example code files for all Packt books you have purchased from your account at http://www.packtpub.com. If you purchased this book elsewhere, you can visit http://www.packtpub.com/support and register to have the files e-mailed directly to you.

Errata

Although we have taken every care to ensure the accuracy of our content, mistakes do happen. If you find a mistake in one of our books—maybe a mistake in the text or the code—we would be grateful if you would report this to us. By doing so, you can save other readers from frustration and help us improve subsequent versions of this book. If you find any errata, please report them by visiting http://www.packtpub.com/submit-errata, selecting your book, clicking on the **errata submission form** link, and entering the details of your errata. Once your errata are verified, your submission will be accepted and the errata will be uploaded on our website, or added to any list of existing errata, under the Errata section of that title. Any existing errata can be viewed by selecting your title from http://www.packtpub.com/support.

Piracy

Piracy of copyright material on the Internet is an ongoing problem across all media. At Packt Publishing, we take the protection of our copyright and licenses very seriously. If you come across any illegal copies of our works, in any form, on the Internet, please provide us with the location address or website name immediately so that we can pursue a remedy.

Please contact us at copyright@packtpub.com with a link to the suspected pirated material.

We appreciate your help in protecting our authors, and our ability to bring you valuable content.

Questions

You can contact us at questions@packtpub.com if you are having a problem with any aspect of the book, and we will do our best to address it.

1
CRUD Operations, Sorting, Filtering, and Joins

Data storage and management have been a very powerful trait for a long time, and as a server-side web developer, it is of paramount importance to have a thorough understanding of the available data storage options. The data that we might be dealing with could be user information, company data, order data, product data, or personal data, and so on. Data in its raw form needs to be processed, cleared, and organized to generate information. Text files and spreadsheets can be used by web applications for storing data but, as the amount of data grows in size, it becomes very hard to store all the data in a single file, as the burgeoning size takes its toll on the speed of retrieval, insertion, and constant updates to the file. Numerous websites store the users' access information in daily or weekly logfiles in the text format, which ends up with a large number of logfiles. The common problem with data storage in this fashion is conserving the data integrity, an example being the process of weeding out duplicate records when data spanned across multiple files becomes cumbersome. A few other problems with data storage in files is the process of managing updates to the file, logging the information about what the updates were or who made them, and applying the necessary file locks when multiple users access and update files at the same time. These are a few reasons why there has always been a need to look for other data storage and management solutions.

An alternate data storage solution, the method that we will rely upon for the most part of this book, is to store the data in a database. A database is an integrated collection of data, and the rules pertaining to that data. A database relies upon a database management system to store the data in an organized manner, to implement the rules that guard the data, and to make the operations such as data retrieval, data modification, and data management simple.

A **Database Management System (DBMS)** is a software or a collection of programs that manage a single database or multiple databases, and provide critical functionality for data administration, data access, and efficient data security. An example of a database management system is a bookshelf, which is an enclosed space that can be used for storing books in an organized manner. There are multiple vendors who provide different database management systems and we will focus on MariaDB.

Continuing with the bookshelf example, the content of a book is divided into chapters; similarly, the data in a database is stored in tables. A table can be described as the fundamental building block of the database. Data can only be stored inside a table, if there are no tables in the database; the database is devoid of data. Every table is identified by a unique name, meaning that the same database cannot have two tables with the same name. The data in a table is stored and is represented in a two-dimensional format as rows and columns. MariaDB is a RDBMS and follows the theory of relational-models proposed by Edgar F Codd. The term *relational* is applied in two ways, the first is the relation between one or more tables in the same database and the second is the relationship between the columns within a table.

Tables carry certain characteristics and are built based on a specific structure (or a layout) that defines how the data will be stored. These characteristics are a unique name for the column and the type of data that will be stored in the column. A row would store the smallest unit of information that can be stored in a table and each column in the table will store a piece of relevant data for a single record. We can have a table with all our users' data, a table with all our orders information, and a table with all our product information. Here, each row in the users table would represent a user record, each row in the orders table would represent an order record, and each row in the products table would represent a product record. In the users table, the columns could be username, address, city, state, and zip code; all these columns provide certain data about the user. Each column is associated with a datatype that defines the type of data that can be stored in the column. Datatypes restrict the type of data that can be stored in a column, which allows for a more efficient storage of data. Based on the type of data that is expected to be stored, datatypes can be broadly categorized into numeric, string, and date-time datatypes.

String datatypes

Let us look at the following main datatypes:

Datatype	Explanation	Comments
CHAR(L)	This stores a fixed-length string between 0 and 255 bytes.	Trailing spaces are removed.
VARCHAR(L)	This stores a variable-length string between 0 and 65,535 characters.	65,535 is the effective maximum row size for table.
TEXT	This stores character data and the maximum length of a text column is 65,535 characters.	Length need not be specified.
TINYTEXT	This stores the text column with a maximum length of 255 characters.	
MEDIUMTEXT	This stores the text column with a maximum length of 16,777,215 characters.	
LONGTEXT	This stores the text column with a maximum length of 4,294,967,295 characters.	
BLOB	This stores binary data and the maximum length of a text column is 65,535 bytes.	Binary Large Objects are used to store binary data such as images.
TINYBLOB	The BLOB datatype column with a maximum length of 255 bytes.	
MEDIUMBLOB	This stores the text column with a maximum length of 16,777,215 bytes.	
LONGBLOB	This stores the text column with a maximum length of 4,294,967,295 bytes.	
ENUM	This provides a list of strings from which a value can be chosen.	A list of 65,535 values can be inserted into the ENUM datatype.
SET	This is similar to the ENUM datatype. It provides a list of strings from which zero or more values can be chosen.	Can have a maximum of 64 distinct values.

Number datatypes

Let us now look at the following main number datatypes:

Datatype	Explanation	Comments
tinyint	This stores integer values.	-128 to 127, Signed 0 to 255, Unsigned
Smallint	This stores integer values.	-32768 to 32767, Signed 0 to 65535, Unsigned
Mediumint	This stores integer values.	-8388608 to 8388607, Signed 0 – 16777215, Unsigned
int(l)	This stores integer values and takes the size of the number.	-2147483648 to 2147483647, Signed 0 – 4294967295, Unsigned
Bigint	This stores integer values.	-9223372036854775808 to 9223372036854775807, Signed 0 to 18446744073709551615, Unsigned
Float(l,d)	This stores floating point numbers and allows us to define the display length (l) and the number of digits after the decimal point (d). The default values for l, d are 10 and 2, respectively.	This uses 4-byte single precision and can display from 0 to 23 digits after the decimal.
Double(l,d)	This is similar to FLOAT, and uses 8-byte double precision. The default values for l, d are 16 and 4, respectively.	The DOUBLE datatype can display from 24 to 53 results. Both the FLOAT and DOUBLE datatypes are commonly used for storing the results from scientific calculations.
decimal(l,d)	This stores the exact numeric data values and allows us to define the display length (l) and the number of digits after decimal point (d).	This is used for precision mathematics that deals with extremely accurate results. The DECIMAL datatype is commonly used to store monetary data.

Date datatypes

Let us now look at the following main date datatypes:

Datatype	Explanation	Comments
Date	This stores the date in YYYY-MM-DD format.	The supported range is from 1000-01-01 to 9999-12-31.
Time	This stores the time in HHH:MM:SS format.	The supported range is from -838:59:59 to 838:59:59.
datetime	This stores both the date and time in YYYY-MM-DD HH:MM:SS format.	The supported range is from 1000-01-01 00:00:00 to 9999-12-31 23:59:59.
Timestamp	This stores both the date and time.	The supported range is from 1970-01-01 00:00:01 UTC to 2038-01-19 03:14:07 UTC.
year (L)	This stores the year in either a 2-digit or a 4-digit format. The length of the year can be specified during declaration. The default is a 4-digit year.	The supported range for a 4-digit year is from 1901 to 2155.

Now that we have discussed the available datatypes for building columns, we will use SQL to build our first table. **Structured Query Language (SQL)** is a multipurpose programming language that allows us to communicate with the database management system to manage and perform operations on the data. SQL operations can be divided into three groups: **Data Definition Language (DDL)**, **Data Manipulation Language (DML)**, and **Data Control Language (DCL)**. These three groups are explained in the following table:

Groups	Explanation	Operations
DDL	Data Definition Language can be used to create a table or alter the structure of a table once it is built, drop the table if it is deemed to be unnecessary, and to perform operations such as truncating the data in a table and creating and dropping indexes on columns.	• CREATE • ALTER • DROP • TRUNCATE • RENAME

Groups	Explanation	Operations
DML	Data Manipulation Language is used to perform insert, update, delete, and select operations on the data.	• SELECT • INSERT • UPDATE • DELETE • CALL • REPLACE • LOAD DATA INFILE
DCL	Data Control Language is used for managing the access to the data. DCL can be used to work with MariaDB's complex security model.	• GRANT • REVOKE
Other administration and utility statements	Other SQL commands that are often used but do not come under DDL, DML, or DCL.	• EXPLAIN • SHOW • DESCRIBE • HELP • USE

Now that we have discussed the basics of Database Management System and SQL, let us connect to our MariaDB server. MariaDB is shipped with a few pre-existing databases that are used by MariaDB itself to store metadata such as information about databases, tables, columns, users, privileges, logs, and so on (yes, MariaDB stores its own data in MariaDB tables).

 For more information about the installation procedures for PHP, MariaDB, and Apache, please refer to the *Bonus chapter 1, Installation of PHP, MariaDB, and Apache* present online on the Packt Publishing website.

As we have installed MariaDB and have root access to the server, we will be able to view all this metadata information. To retrieve the metadata information that is currently on MariaDB, we will use the SHOW utility command and, as we are interested in retrieving the list of existing databases, we will append DATABASES to our SHOW command:

```
MariaDB [(none)]> show databases;
+--------------------+
| Database           |
+--------------------+
| information_schema |
| mysql              |
| performance_schema |
+--------------------+
3 rows in set (0.00 sec)
```

 SQL commands are case-insensitive, so the case of the SQL command does not matter.

Upon executing the show databases; command, the list of existing databases will be outputted to the screen. These databases are reserved to store configurations and necessary metadata (yes, MariaDB stores its data on MariaDB itself), so it is advised to avoid using these databases for storing other data. For storing other data, we will have to create our own database. We will use the SQL commands that are part of DDL to create new databases. For creating a new database, the CREATE DDL command is appended with DATABASE and then the name of the database to be created is added. Let us create a simple course registry database that keeps a track of student records, the available courses, and the courses for which the students have registered.

 MariaDB is very particular about statement terminators, a semicolon ; is the default statement terminator and, unless the statement terminator is given, the SQL command is not executed.

```
MariaDB [(none)]> create database course_registry;
Query OK, 1 row affected (0.00 sec)
```

We have successfully created our first database. To verify that we have created this database, let us run the `show databases;` command one more time to see if our new database is reflected in the list of existing databases:

```
MariaDB [(none)]> show databases;
+--------------------+
| Database           |
+--------------------+
| information_schema |
| course_registry    |
| mysql              |
| performance_schema |
+--------------------+
4 rows in set (0.00 sec)
```

Now that we have verified that our new database is available in the list of existing databases, let us access the database and build tables in the `course_registry` database. For accessing a database, we will utilize the USE utility command. The USE command has to be followed with the name of an existing database to avoid an error, once this command has been executed.

```
MariaDB [(none)]> use course_registry;
Database changed
MariaDB [course_registry]> █
```

Now that the database has been successfully changed, note that the database name reflects in between the brackets next to **MariaDB**, which denotes the current database.

 Another way of finding the current database is to use the `select database();` statement and print it out to the console; if the output is null, this means that no database has been selected.

Now that we have chosen the `course_registry` database, let us take a brief look at the data that has to be housed in this database. The `course_registry` database keeps a track of student records, the available courses, and the courses for which the students have registered. We could do this by putting the students and the courses that they have registered for in a single table. However, the problems with this approach, similar to a spreadsheet, are twofold. The first problem is that the student information would keep repeating when a student registers for multiple courses, thereby causing unnecessary redundancy.

The second problem will be about data inconsistency, assuming that the student information was wrong. Either we will be using this erroneous information another time, or we might be employing another data entry process that allows the user to enter different data as user information, which causes data inconsistency. To avoid this, we are splitting our data into three tables; they are students, courses, and students_courses.

The student records will be stored in the students table, the data about the available courses will be stored in the courses table, and the data about the courses that the students have registered for will be stored in the students_courses table. The students_courses table will be an association table that contains common fields from the students and the courses tables. This table can also be referred to as a *bridge table*, *paired table*, or *cross reference* table. By using the students_courses table, we can accommodate a common case where one student can register for more than one course.

Before we begin building our tables, it is always important to understand the type data that will be housed in this table and based on the data that will be housed in that table, we will have to decide on the column names and the datatypes for those columns. Column names have to be intuitive in order to help others such as system administrators, auditors, and fellow developers to easily understand the kind of data that can be or is currently being stored in those columns, and the respective datatypes of those columns will explain the type that can be housed in a column. Let us begin with our students table.

The students table

Let us take a look at the following fields in the table and what work they perform:

Column name	Datatype	Comments
student_id	Int	This stores the unique identifier for a student
first_name	Varchar(60)	This stores the first name of the student
last_name	Varchar(60)	This stores the last name of the student
address	Varchar(255)	This stores the address of the student
city	Varchar(45)	This stores the name of the city
state	Char(2)	This stores the two letter abbreviation for states in the United States
zip_code	Char(5)	This stores the five digit zip code for an address in the United States

It is advised to use a character datatype for fields such as zip codes or SSNs. Though the data is going to be a number, integer datatypes are notorious for removing preceding zeroes, so if there is a zip code that starts with a zero, such as 06909, of an integer datatype, the zip code would end up in the column as 6909.

Now let us convert this table structure into executable SQL, to create our table, we will be using the CREATE DDL command, followed by TABLE and then append it with the table structure. In SQL, the column description is done by mentioning the column name first and then adding the datatype of the column. The STUDENTS table has multiple columns, and the column information has to be separated by a comma (,).

```
MariaDB [course_registry]> create table students(
    -> student_id int,
    -> first_name varchar(60),
    -> last_name varchar(60),
    -> address varchar(255),
    -> city varchar(40),
    -> state char(2),
    -> zip_code char(5)
    -> );
Query OK, 0 rows affected (0.05 sec)
```

Now that the query has been executed, the students table has been created. To verify if the students table has been successfully built, and to view a list of existing tables that are in the current database, we can use the SHOW utility command and append that with TABLES:

```
MariaDB [course_registry]> show tables;
+-----------------------+
| Tables_in_course_registry |
+-----------------------+
| students              |
+-----------------------+
1 row in set (0.00 sec)
```

We have successfully used the show tables; command SQL statement to retrieve a list of existing tables, and have verified that our students table exists in our course_registry database. Now, let us verify if our students table has the same table structure as we originally intended it to have. We will use the DESCRIBE utility command followed by the table name to understand the table structure:

The DESCRIBE and DESC commands can be used interchangeably, both the commands would need the table name to return their structure.

```
MariaDB [course_registry]> describe students;
+------------+--------------+------+-----+---------+-------+
| Field      | Type         | Null | Key | Default | Extra |
+------------+--------------+------+-----+---------+-------+
| student_id | int(11)      | YES  |     | NULL    |       |
| first_name | varchar(60)  | YES  |     | NULL    |       |
| last_name  | varchar(60)  | YES  |     | NULL    |       |
| address    | varchar(255) | YES  |     | NULL    |       |
| city       | varchar(40)  | YES  |     | NULL    |       |
| state      | char(2)      | YES  |     | NULL    |       |
| zip_code   | char(5)      | YES  |     | NULL    |       |
+------------+--------------+------+-----+---------+-------+
7 rows in set (0.00 sec)
```

Now let us move on to the `courses` table, this table will house all the available courses for which a student can register. The courses table will contain a unique identifier for the course (`course_id`), the name of the course (`course_name`), and a brief description of the course (`course_description`).

The courses table

Let us now look at the fields and the type of values they are storing:

Column name	Datatype	Comments
course_id	int	This stores the unique identifier for a course.
name	varchar(60)	This stores the title of the course.
description	varchar(255)	This stores the description of a course.

Now let us convert this table structure into executable SQL to create our `courses` table:

```
MariaDB [course_registry]> create table courses(
    -> course_id int,
    -> name varchar(60),
    -> description varchar(255)
    -> );
Query OK, 0 rows affected (0.08 sec)
```

Now that the query has been executed, let us run the SHOW TABLES command to verify if the courses table has been created:

```
MariaDB [course_registry]> show tables;
+-------------------------+
| Tables_in_course_registry |
+-------------------------+
| courses                 |
| students                |
+-------------------------+
2 rows in set (0.00 sec)
```

The output from the SHOW TABLES command returns the list of current tables, and the courses table is one of them. Now that we have built the students table and the courses table, let us build the bridge table that would hold the association between the two tables. This table would contain the data about the students who were enrolled to a particular course.

The students_courses table

Let us now look at the fields in this table and their respective values:

Column name	Datatype	Comments
course_id	int	This stores the unique identifier for a course
student_id	int	This stores the unique identifier for a student

Now, let us convert this table structure into executable SQL, to create our courses table using the following command:

```
MariaDB [course_registry]> create table students_courses(
    -> course_id int,
    -> student_id int
    -> );
Query OK, 0 rows affected (0.01 sec)
```

Now that the query has been executed, let us run the SHOW TABLES command to verify if the courses table has been created:

```
MariaDB [course_registry]> show tables;
+--------------------------+
| Tables_in_course_registry |
+--------------------------+
| courses                  |
| students                 |
| students_courses         |
+--------------------------+
3 rows in set (0.00 sec)
```

The output from the SHOW TABLES command returns the list of current tables, and the students_courses table is one of them.

Inserting data

Now that we have built our tables, it is time to insert records into the tables.

Let us look at a few different methods for inserting a single row of data and inserting multiple rows of data. For insertion of data into a table, we will use the INSERT DML command, and supply the table name and the values for the available columns in the table. Let us begin by inserting student records into the students table:

```
MariaDB [course_registry]> insert into students
    -> values( 1,
    -> "John",
    -> "Doe",
    -> "3225 Woodland Park St",
    -> "Houston",
    -> "TX",
    -> "77082"
    -> );
Query OK, 1 row affected (0.10 sec)
```

In this example, we insert a new student record into the students table; we are supplying the data for that student record in the VALUES clause. This syntax, though it appears to be very simple, it is not a very safe method of inserting data. This INSERT statement is depending upon the order in which the columns were defined in the table structure, so the data in the VALUES clause will be mapped by position, 1 would go into the first column in the table, though it is intended to go into the student_id column. If the students table is rebuilt locally or on a different machine, there is no guarantee that the column order would remain the same as the order on the current MariaDB database server. The other approach that is considered safer when compared to this one is the INSERT statement, where the column names are explicitly mentioned in the SQL:

```
MariaDB [course_registry]> insert into students(
    -> student_id,
    -> first_name,
    -> last_name,
    -> address,
    -> city,
    -> state,
    -> zip_code
    -> )
    -> values( 2,
    -> "Jane",
    -> "Dane",
    -> "49 Puritan Ln",
    -> "Stamford",
    -> "CT",
    -> "06906"
    -> );
Query OK, 1 row affected (0.11 sec)
```

Though this might be a bit longer, this would guarantee that data that is being passed in via the VALUES clause is going into the right column. By using this INSERT syntax, the order in which the columns are mentioned is no longer important. When this query is executed, MariaDB matches each item in the columns list with its respective value in the VALUES list by position. This syntax can also be used for the case where the data is only available for a few columns. Let us come up with an INSERT statement that has data for a few columns and uses NULL for a column that does not have any data:

 In SQL, the term NULL is used to denote that a value does not exist.

```
MariaDB [course_registry]> insert into students(
    -> student_id,
    -> first_name,
    -> last_name,
    -> address,
    -> city,
    -> state,
    -> zip_code
    -> )
    -> values( 3,
    -> "Richard",
    -> "Roe",
    -> NULL,
    -> "Atlanta",
    -> "GA",
    -> "30328"
    -> );
Query OK, 1 row affected (0.14 sec)
```

In this example, we are inserting a student record whose `address` is not known, so we are using NULL to populate the column.

 Columns by default allow NULL values to be populated, unless it is explicitly mentioned not to allow NULL values.

Now that we have seen the different insertion syntaxes for inserting a single record row, let us take a step forward and look at how multiple records can be inserted. There are two ways of inserting multiple records into a table, the first method is where INSERT statements are created for each row, and are separated by the statement terminator (;):

```
insert into courses(
        course_id, name, description
)
values(1, "CS-101",
        "Introduction to Computer Science");

insert into courses(
        course_id, name, description
)
values(2, "CE-101",
        "Introduction to Computer Engineering");
```

The other way of inserting multiple records is by using a single VALUES clause while passing in multiple records, separating each record with a comma (,), and adding a statement terminator at the end of the last record:

```
insert into students_courses(
        student_id, course_id)
values
        (1,1), -- Student id 1 & Course id 1
        (1,2), -- Student id 1 & Course id 2
        (2,2), -- Student id 2 & Course id 2
        (3,1); -- Student id 3 & Course id 1
```

We are currently not using any constraints to maintain any referential integrity among tables, so any integers can be inserted into the students_courses table. To allow only existing student IDs and course IDs to be inserted, we will have to use the primary key and foreign key constraints. We will be covering constraints in the next chapter.

In this example, we are inserting multiple records into the students_courses table. On execution of this SQL query, the first statement inserts an associative record into the students_courses table and the value for the column student_id is 1, which maps back to the student record of John Doe, and the value for course_id is 1 that corresponds to the course record CS-101. The inline comments at the end of each statement are used to describe the data that is being inserted via this statement. Though these comments are added to the INSERT statements, they are only intended to explain the purpose of the statements and will not be processed by MariaDB.

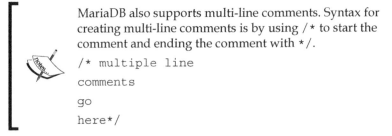

MariaDB also supports multi-line comments. Syntax for creating multi-line comments is by using /* to start the comment and ending the comment with */.

```
/* multiple line
comments
go
here*/
```

The last method of insertion that we are skipping for now is to insert the data that has been retrieved on the fly from a table. We will be looking at that once we have covered the methods for retrieving data and filtering data.

Retrieving data

Now that we have inserted data into the `students`, `courses`, and `students_courses` tables, let us look at the different mechanisms of retrieving data, we will be using the `SELECT` command to retrieve the data. The `SELECT` statement would expect two things as a minimum, the first would be what to retrieve and the second would be where to retrieve it. The simplest `SELECT` command would be to retrieve all the student records from the students table:

```
MariaDB [course_registry]> select * from students;
+------------+------------+-----------+----------------------+----------+-------+----------+
| student_id | first_name | last_name | address              | city     | state | zip_code |
+------------+------------+-----------+----------------------+----------+-------+----------+
|          1 | John       | Doe       | 3225 Woodland Park St | Houston  | TX    | 77082    |
|          2 | Jane       | Dane      | 49 Puritan Ln        | Stamford | CT    | 06906    |
|          3 | Richard    | Roe       | NULL                 | Atlanta  | GA    | 30328    |
+------------+------------+-----------+----------------------+----------+-------+----------+
3 rows in set (0.00 sec)
```

In this query, we are using `*` to retrieve the data for all the columns from the students table, this is not a preferred method of retrieving data. The preferred method for data retrieval is by mentioning the individual columns separated by a comma (`,`) after the `SELECT` clause:

```
MariaDB [course_registry]> select student_id, first_name,
    -> last_name from students;
+------------+------------+-----------+
| student_id | first_name | last_name |
+------------+------------+-----------+
|          1 | John       | Doe       |
|          2 | Jane       | Dane      |
|          3 | Richard    | Roe       |
+------------+------------+-----------+
3 rows in set (0.00 sec)
```

In this query, we are selecting the `student_id`, `first_name`, and `last_name` columns from the `students` table. As we are not filtering the data yet, `SELECT` statements would return every student record that is in the students table. We can use the `LIMIT` clause to retrieve a certain number of records:

```
MariaDB [course_registry]> select student_id, first_name,
    -> last_name from students limit 1;
+------------+------------+-----------+
| student_id | first_name | last_name |
+------------+------------+-----------+
|          1 | John       | Doe       |
+------------+------------+-----------+
1 row in set (0.00 sec)
```

In this query, we are retrieving the data from the `students` table and we are retrieving the `student_id`, `first_name`, and `last_name` columns; however, rather than retrieving all the rows, we are only retrieving a single row. To retrieve the next row, we could still use the limit, but we would use `LIMIT` clause accompanied by the `OFFSET` clause. The `OFFSET` clause determines the starting point as to where the records should start from, while the `LIMIT` clause determines the number of records that would be retrieved.

Sorting data

Now that we have looked at different techniques of retrieving the data, let us look at how the data can be represented in a more ordered way. When we execute a `SELECT` statement, the data is retrieved in the order in which it exists in the database. This would be the order in which the data is stored; therefore, it is not a good idea to depend upon MariaDB's default sorting. MariaDB provides an explicit mechanism for sorting data; we can use the `ORDER BY` clause with the `SELECT` statement and sort the data as needed. To understand how sorting can be of help, let us begin by querying the `students` table and only retrieving the `first_name` column:

```
MariaDB [course_registry]> select first_name from students;
+------------+
| first_name |
+------------+
| John       |
| Jane       |
| Richard    |
+------------+
3 rows in set (0.00 sec)
```

In the first example, we are going by MariaDB's default sort, and this would give us the data that is being returned based on the order of the insert:

```
MariaDB [course_registry]> select first_name from students
    -> order by first_name;
+------------+
| first_name |
+------------+
| Jane       |
| John       |
| Richard    |
+------------+
3 rows in set (0.00 sec)
```

In this example, we are ordering the data based on the first_name column. The ORDER BY clause by default sorts in ascending order, so the data would be sorted in an ascending alphabetical order and if the first character of one or more strings is the same, then the data is sorted by the second character, which is why Jane comes before John. To explicitly mention the sort order as ascending, we can use the keyword asc after the column name:

```
MariaDB [course_registry]> select first_name from students
    -> order by first_name desc;
+------------+
| first_name |
+------------+
| Richard    |
| John       |
| Jane       |
+------------+
3 rows in set (0.00 sec)
```

In this example, we are again ordering the data based on the first_name column and the ORDER BY clause has been supplied with desc, we are setting the sort direction to descending, which denotes that the data has been sorted in a descending order. MariaDB also provides a multi-column sort, which is a sort within a sort. To perform a multi-column sort, we would specify the column names after the ORDER BY clause separated by comma (,). The way the multi-column works is, the data would be first sorted by the first column that is mentioned in the ORDER BY clause, and then the dataset that has already been sorted by the first column is again sorted by the next column and the data is returned back. As a muti-column sort performs sorting on multiple levels, the order of columns will determine the way the data is ordered. To perform this example, let us insert another row with the student name **John Dane** and the student ID being 4, the reason for using **John Dane** is to make sure that there are more than one students that share the first name of **John** (**John Doe** and **John Dane**) and the last name of **Dane** (**Jane Dane** and **John Dane**) exclusively:

```
MariaDB [course_registry]> select last_name, first_name from students
    -> order by last_name, first_name;
+-----------+------------+
| last_name | first_name |
+-----------+------------+
| Dane      | Jane       |
| Dane      | John       |
| Doe       | John       |
| Roe       | Richard    |
+-----------+------------+
4 rows in set (0.00 sec)
```

In this example, we are retrieving the `last_name` and `first_name` columns from the `students` table and are first ordering the data by "last_name" and then reordering the previously ordered dataset by `first_name`. We are not restricted by the ORDER BY clause to use only the columns being used for the sort. This will only help us sort the data in the correct direction.

Filtering data

Until now, we have dealt with data retrieval where all the data in the `students` table is being retrieved, but seldom do we need all that data. We have used the LIMIT and OFFSET clauses that have allowed us to limit the amount of data were retrieved. Now let us use MariaDB's filtering mechanism to retrieve the data by supplying search criteria. To perform a search in a SQL statement, we will use the WHERE clause. The WHERE clause can be used with the SELECT statement, or it can be even used with the UPDATE and DELETE statements, which will be discussed in the next section:

```
MariaDB [course_registry]> select student_id, first_name, last_name
    -> from students
    -> where last_name="Dane";
+------------+------------+-----------+
| student_id | first_name | last_name |
+------------+------------+-----------+
|          2 | Jane       | Dane      |
|          4 | John       | Dane      |
+------------+------------+-----------+
2 rows in set (0.00 sec)
```

In the preceding example, we are selecting the students' records whose `last_name` is Dane.

```
MariaDB [course_registry]> select student_id, first_name, last_name
    -> from students
    -> where student_id=1;
+------------+------------+-----------+
| student_id | first_name | last_name |
+------------+------------+-----------+
|          1 | John       | Doe       |
+------------+------------+-----------+
1 row in set (0.00 sec)
```

In the preceding example, we are selecting the students' records whose
`student_id` is 1.

```
MariaDB [course_registry]> select student_id, first_name, last_name
    -> from students
    -> where student_id>1;
+------------+------------+-----------+
| student_id | first_name | last_name |
+------------+------------+-----------+
|          2 | Jane       | Dane      |
|          3 | Richard    | Roe       |
|          4 | John       | Dane      |
+------------+------------+-----------+
3 rows in set (0.00 sec)
```

In the preceding example, we are selecting the students' records whose
`student_id` is greater than 1.

```
MariaDB [course_registry]> select student_id, first_name, last_name
    -> from students
    -> where student_id<4;
+------------+------------+-----------+
| student_id | first_name | last_name |
+------------+------------+-----------+
|          1 | John       | Doe       |
|          2 | Jane       | Dane      |
|          3 | Richard    | Roe       |
+------------+------------+-----------+
3 rows in set (0.00 sec)
```

In the preceding example, we are selecting the students' records whose
`student_id` is less than 4.

```
MariaDB [course_registry]> select student_id, first_name, last_name
    -> from students
    -> where student_id between 1 and 4;
+------------+------------+-----------+
| student_id | first_name | last_name |
+------------+------------+-----------+
|          1 | John       | Doe       |
|          2 | Jane       | Dane      |
|          3 | Richard    | Roe       |
|          4 | John       | Dane      |
+------------+------------+-----------+
4 rows in set (0.00 sec)
```

In the preceding example, we are selecting the students' records whose `student_id` is between 1 and 4, the between clause is inclusive, so the records with `student_id` 1 and 4 are also retrieved. The following table lists the common operators that can be used for data filtering:

Operator	Explanation	Comment
=	Filters and returns data where the criterion has an exact match.	
!=	Filters and returns data where the criterion doesn't have an exact match.	
<>	Filters and returns data where the criterion doesn't have an exact match.	This is same as above, based on preference, either notations can be used for inequality.
>	Filters and returns data where the data is greater than the value in the criterion.	
>=	Filters and returns data where the data is greater than or equal to the value in the criterion.	
<	Filters and returns data where the data is lesser than the value in the criterion.	
<=	Filters and returns data where the data is lesser than or equal to the criterion.	
IS NULL	Filters and returns the rows where the specified column has no data.	
IS NOT NULL	Filters and returns the rows where the specified column has some data.	
BETWEEN	Filters and returns data where the data is part of the specified range.	This uses the keywords BETWEEN, and AND.

Data can also be filtered by utilizing multiple search criteria by using the AND and OR operators, by employing multiple column search criteria, by using wildcard filtering, by using the IN operator, and so on. As this chapter will only deal with basic filtering, we will not be covering these advanced filtering concepts. The basic filtering in this chapter can be used as a foundation to delve deeper into understanding the advanced concepts of filtering.

Updating data

Until now, we have worked with the creation of databases, tables, data, and retrieval of data. Now let us go over the process of updating data, once the data has been added to the table, there will be different cases where the data has to be updated, such as a typo while adding the student's name, or if the student's address changes after they have registered for the course, and so on. We will use the UPDATE DML statement to modify the data. The UPDATE statement requires a minimum of three details, the first is the name of the table on which this operation will be performed, the second is the name of the column, and the third is the value that the column to has to be assigned to. We can also use the UPDATE statement to modify more than one column at a time. There are two cases where the UPDATE statement can be used. The first case is where all the records in the table will be updated, and this has to be done very carefully as this could cause the loss of existing data. The second scenario when using the UPDATE statement is in combination with the WHERE clause. By using the WHERE clause, we are targeting a very specific set of records based on the filter criteria.

 It is recommended to execute the filter criteria with a SELECT statement, so that we can verify the dataset on which our UPDATE statement would run, in order to make any required changes if the filter criterion does not reflect the expected results. Another way of handling such scenarios is to use a transaction, which will allow us to rollback any changes that we have made.

```
MariaDB [course_registry]> update students
    -> set city = "Lincoln"
    -> where student_id = 4;
Query OK, 1 row affected (0.11 sec)
Rows matched: 1  Changed: 1  Warnings: 0
```

In the preceding example, we have updated John Dane's current city to **Nebraska** by using his student ID. We can also verify this by looking at the output on the query console, it returns that the filter criterion was matched for one row, and the update statement was applied for that one row.

Deleting data

We will use the DELETE DML statement for deletion of data. The DELETE statement at a minimum expects the name of the table. Similar to the UPDATE statement, it is recommended that the DELETE statement is always used with filter criteria to avoid loss of data.

The DELETE statement should be used when a record has to be permanently removed from the table.

 To avoid permanent loss or deletion of data Boolean flags are used to determine if a record is active or inactive (1 or 0). These are called soft deletes and help us retain data in the long run.

```
MariaDB [course_registry]> delete from students
    -> where student_id=4;
Query OK, 1 row affected (0.11 sec)
```

In the preceding example, we are deleting the records from the students table that match the criterion of student_id equal to 4. As there is only one record that matches that criterion, that record has been deleted. The recommendations that were made above about how to use the filter criterion apply for the DELETE statement too.

Joins

Until now, we have coupled our SELECT statements with various filtering and sorting techniques to query the student information extensively. As we are operating in a relational-model of data storage and since our data is stored in different tables, we are yet to figure out how our SELECT statements can be fired across multiple tables. In our case, this would help us find out what course or courses a student has registered for, or to find our which course has the most number of students. Following the relational-model of data allows us to store data in a more efficient manner, allows us to independently manipulate the data in different tables, and allows for greater scalability; however, querying the data across multiple tables is going to be difficult when compared to retrieving records from a single table. We will use JOINS to associate multiple tables, to retrieve, update, or delete data.

A SQL JOIN is a virtual entity and is performed at run time, during the execution of the SQL statement. Similar to any other SQL statement, the data would only be available during the query execution and is not implicitly persisted to the disk. A SQL JOIN can be coupled with a SELECT statement to retrieve data from multiple tables. Let us go through the most common JOIN: the INNER JOIN, a join based on the equality comparison on the join-predicate.

Let us look at a few examples that perform SQL INNER JOIN between two or more tables:

```
MariaDB [course_registry]> select students.first_name,
    -> students.last_name,
    -> students_courses.course_id
    -> from students
    -> inner join
    -> students_courses
    -> on
    -> students.student_id
    -> =
    -> students_courses.student_id;
+------------+-----------+-----------+
| first_name | last_name | course_id |
+------------+-----------+-----------+
| John       | Doe       |         1 |
| John       | Doe       |         2 |
| Jane       | Dane      |         2 |
| Richard    | Roe       |         1 |
+------------+-----------+-----------+
4 rows in set (0.00 sec)
```

In the preceding example, we are joining the students and students_courses tables to retrieve a list of all the students who have registered for a course. This is similar to the SELECT statements that we worked with earlier; a big difference is that we can now add a column that is part of a different table. We use the INNER JOIN clause to build the association between students and the students_courses table where the values for student_id in the students table exist in the students_courses table; this is referred to as the join-predicate. Now let us join all the tables and retrieve the names of the courses for which each student has registered.

```
MariaDB [course_registry]> select students.first_name,
    -> students.last_name,
    -> courses.name as course_name
    -> from students
    -> inner join
    -> students_courses on
    -> students.student_id = students_courses.student_id
    -> inner join
    -> courses on
    -> students_courses.course_id = courses.course_id;
+------------+-----------+-------------+
| first_name | last_name | course_name |
+------------+-----------+-------------+
| John       | Doe       | CS-101      |
| John       | Doe       | CE-101      |
| Jane       | Dane      | CE-101      |
| Richard    | Roe       | CS-101      |
+------------+-----------+-------------+
4 rows in set (0.00 sec)
```

In this example, we are creating an alias name for the name column in the courses table. We are using the AS statement to explicitly create a temporary alias to make the column name more intuitive. We can build aliases for tables in a similar manner

In the previous example, we have joined the three tables that are available in our course_registry database and are now able to retrieve the list of courses for which the students have registered. Similar to our previous SELECT statements, let us add a filter criterion to narrow down our search:

```
MariaDB [course_registry]> select students.first_name,
    -> students.last_name,
    -> courses.name as course_name
    -> from students
    -> inner join
    -> students_courses on
    -> students.student_id = students_courses.student_id
    -> inner join
    -> courses on
    -> students_courses.course_id = courses.course_id
    -> where students.student_id = 2; -- Jane Dane
+------------+-----------+-------------+
| first_name | last_name | course_name |
+------------+-----------+-------------+
| Jane       | Dane      | CE-101      |
+------------+-----------+-------------+
1 row in set (0.00 sec)
```

In the preceding example, we are filtering the data by student_id and are searching for records with student_id equal to 2. We have discussed the most commonly used form JOIN statement, which is the INNER JOIN or the equi-join. There are other types of JOIN in SQL that are supported by MariaDB such as OUTER JOIN, SELF JOIN, and NATURAL JOIN, we will be skipping these JOIN statements.

Summary

In this chapter, we have covered the basics of relational database management systems with MariaDB. We began by building our first database, and performed **Create**, **Read**, **Update**, and **Delete** (**CRUD**) operations. We used the SQL SELECT statement to retrieve data and used the ORDER BY and WHERE statements to sort and filter the data respectively. Later, we moved on to use the UPDATE and DELETE statements to modify and remove data respectively. Finally, we used the INNER JOIN to retrieve data from multiple tables and coupled that with the WHERE statement to filter that data.

In the next chapter, we will be going over more advanced topics such as creating calculated fields and building complex views, stored procedures, functions, and triggers.

2
Advanced Programming with MariaDB

In the previous chapter, we have discussed basic operations that can be performed on MariaDB such as creating databases and tables, adding data, modifying data, deleting data, and retrieving the data. We have also worked with the basic techniques of sorting and filtering data in order to work with the targeted and specific datasets. In this chapter, we will work with the following advanced concepts:

- Indexes
- Stored procedures
- Functions
- Triggers

Enhancing the existing tables

Let's begin by making a few changes to the existing `students` table. We will be adding two columns to the `students` table that would store a student's username and password. This database will be used to support `Student Portal` that we will build at a later point. The information available in the **username** and **password** fields will be used to authenticate and authorize the student to login to the student portal. There are a couple of ways to facilitate these changes; the first method is to use the `DROP TABLE` DDL command to remove the existing `students` table and use the `CREATE TABLE` DDL command to create a new `students` table that would have the extra `username` and `password` fields. This method however causes loss of existing data. The second method is to use the `ALTER TABLE` DDL command to add new columns to the existing `students` table.

The following screenshot shows the usage of these commands for altering the students table:

```
MariaDB [course_registry]> alter table students
    -> add column username varchar(45) not null,
    -> add column password varchar(40) not null;
Query OK, 13 rows affected (0.76 sec)
Records: 13  Duplicates: 0  Warnings: 0
```

In this example, we have coupled the ALTER TABLE command with the ADD COLUMN SQL command for adding new columns; we have separated the column definitions with a comma (,). We are adding NOT NULL to the end of the column definition to denote that these columns cannot carry null values. Now that we have added these columns, it's time to populate the usernames and passwords for the existing students. It is always recommended to store passwords in a hashed state in order to provide security to the data and the users. We will use the **SHA1** hashing algorithm to hash the passwords, as shown in the following screenshot:

```
MariaDB [course_registry]> select SHA1("anystring");
+------------------------------------------+
| SHA1("anystring")                        |
+------------------------------------------+
| a1c237468569e4e12c7549fc2cc4d9aeb440577f |
+------------------------------------------+
1 row in set (0.00 sec)
```

MariaDB provides a built-in function for generating a **SHA1** hash value for a string. As SHA1 is a static algorithm, it will produce the same hash as long as the same string is provided. As SHA1 is a function by itself, we will have to use subqueries to retrieve the encrypted string. Let's take a step back and look at an example as to how to use subqueries as part of the regular SQL statements. Subqueries are SQL statements that are nested within an existing SQL statement.

Let's use a subquery to retrieve the first name and last name of a student who has registered for the course CS-101 as shown in the following screenshot:

```
MariaDB [course_registry]> select * from courses; --get a list of all courses
+-----------+--------+--------------------------------------+
| course_id | name   | description                          |
+-----------+--------+--------------------------------------+
|         1 | CS-101 | Introduction to Computer Science     |
|         2 | CE-101 | Introduction to Computer Engineering |
+-----------+--------+--------------------------------------+
2 rows in set (0.00 sec)

MariaDB [course_registry]> select student_id from students_courses
    -> where course_id=1 limit 1;--get the first student's id who registered for CS-101
+------------+
| student_id |
+------------+
|          1 |
+------------+
1 row in set (0.00 sec)

MariaDB [course_registry]> select first_name, last_name from students
    -> where student_id=(select student_id from students_courses
    -> where course_id=1 limit 1); --get the firstname and lastname of the student who registered for CS-101
+------------+-----------+
| first_name | last_name |
+------------+-----------+
| John       | Doe       |
+------------+-----------+
1 row in set (0.00 sec)
```

In the preceding example, we start with looking at all the available courses and get student_id of the first student registered for the CS-101 course having course_id as 1. Now we can use the output of this subquery as the value for the filter criterion on the outer SQL statement. We will use this functionality in our update queries to add the usernames and passwords for the existing students. We can also use an INNER JOIN coupled with WHERE to retrieve the output of this query. The purpose of this example is to introduce the readers to the concept of subqueries that will be used to execute the SHA1 function.

 We will be following the convention of having the "firstname.lastname" pattern for a username and the "firstnamelastname" pattern for a password. This pattern for the passwords is being used to keep the examples simple and is not recommended in real-time scenarios.

Consider the example as shown in the following screenshot:

```
MariaDB [course_registry]> update students set username="john.doe",
password=(select SHA1("johndoe")) where student_id=1;
Query OK, 0 rows affected, 2 warnings (0.07 sec)
Rows matched: 1  Changed: 0  Warnings: 2

MariaDB [course_registry]> update students set username="jane.dane",
 password=(select SHA1("janedane")) where student_id=2;
Query OK, 0 rows affected, 2 warnings (0.07 sec)
Rows matched: 1  Changed: 0  Warnings: 2

MariaDB [course_registry]> update students set username="richard.roe
", password=(select SHA1("richardroe")) where student_id=3;
Query OK, 1 row affected, 2 warnings (0.05 sec)
Rows matched: 1  Changed: 1  Warnings: 2
```

We will use the UPDATE DML statement to add the usernames and passwords for the existing users. As discussed earlier, we are using the SHA1 function to hash the passwords. Now that we have added the usernames and passwords, let's look at how the data is stored in the database, as shown in the following screenshot:

```
MariaDB [course_registry]> select first_name, last_name, username, password
    -> from students;
+------------+-----------+-------------+------------------------------------------+
| first_name | last_name | username    | password                                 |
+------------+-----------+-------------+------------------------------------------+
| John       | Doe       | john.doe    | 6579e96f76baa00787a28653876c6127         |
| Jane       | Dane      | jane.dane   | 7f95133e42c00ce84c4dbeb5db326d00         |
| Richard    | Roe       | richard.roe | d6e854df17d6ce05b1dcbdf6fc802f04         |
+------------+-----------+-------------+------------------------------------------+
3 rows in set (0.00 sec)
```

In the preceding example, we are using the SELECT statement to retrieve the first_name, last_name, username, and password fields for the existing users. As we can see in the preceding screenshot, the username is stored as a string and follows our "firstname.lastname" pattern, and the password has been successfully hashed using the SHA1 hashing algorithm.

SHA1 is a one-way hashing algorithm, so the data cannot be converted back into its original format. For our authentication purposes, we will take the student's password, hash it using the SHA1 algorithm, and then compare the password that the student has entered during the login and the password that is in the database.

From the result set that we have retrieved from the SELECT statement used in the previous code, we notice that the data in the username field is unique for all the available columns, but there is no guarantee that another student cannot choose a username that already exists. MariaDB allows adding a **unique key** constraint in order to maintain the uniqueness of the data that is being inserted into the username column. The unique key constraint builds an index in the background to keep track of all the values that are being added to the columns with **unique** constraints.

 As the unique constraints use the unique index, the index looks for the data to be unique; it can also be null. The null value will only hold true for one record.

Let's use the ALTER DDL command to add a unique constraint to the username column in the students table, as shown in the following screenshot:

```
MariaDB [course_registry]> alter table students
    -> add constraint `uk_students_username`
    -> unique(`username`);
Query OK, 0 rows affected (0.28 sec)
Records: 0  Duplicates: 0  Warnings: 0
```

In the preceding example, we are altering the existing students table and combining the ADD CONSTRAINT command to give a user-defined name to the constraint, and then we will be passing the username column to the unique function for creating the unique constraint.

 An alternate method to add a unique index to a column (after the table has been built) is:

```
alter table students add unique 'username'('username');
```

Now that we have created a unique constraint, let's try and see if we can insert a duplicate record. For this example, let's use the username of the student named Richard Roe as shown in the following screenshot:

```
MariaDB [course_registry]> insert into students(username)
    -> values("richard.roe"); --richard.roe already exists
ERROR 1062 (23000): Duplicate entry 'richard.roe' for key 'uk_students_username'
```

Upon execution of this SQL statement, we will receive an error saying that a duplicate entry to be inserted into the username column was entered, which is now protected by the uk_students_username constraint. Assuming that the initial line of SQL code was correct, we would have a student record with the information available only for the username column. In the previous chapter, we discussed that student_id is a unique identifier for students. In order to facilitate this, let's make student_id the primary key of the students table and let MariaDB know that this field always needs a value. A **primary key** is similar to the unique key, except that the primary key does not allow null values. The reason for having null to be an invalid value is that a primary key always identifies each row in a table uniquely. Primary keys are commonly defined in one column, as in our case in student_id; but in other cases, multiple columns can be used to define a primary key. As in our case, it is common to use the non-changing, non-repetitive integer values for the primary keys; as new students are added, we add one to the last student's ID. Currently, we have three students; so, if another student is added, the ID of that student will be 4. We can either do this manually or MariaDB provides an auto-increment functionality that keeps on incrementing the value of the last insert with a default value of 1 or with an incremental value, if the incremental value is provided. The following screenshot shows the usage of the auto_increment function:

```
MariaDB [course_registry]> alter table students
    -> change student_id student_id int not null
    -> auto_increment primary key;
Query OK, 3 rows affected (0.15 sec)
Records: 3  Duplicates: 0  Warnings: 0
```

In the preceding example, we are using the ALTER TABLE DDL command and are combining that with the CHANGE command that allows us to modify the attributes of an existing column. The first change is that the student_id column will not take a null value. Then we are making this column an AUTO INCREMENT column, which that will automatically assign the next available number to the student_id column.

Finally, we are creating a primary key on the student_id column to make sure that the IDs of the students will always be unique and not carry a null value. The next step will be to alter the table one more time and make sure that the value for next student_id will be 4, as we already have three students as shown in the following screenshot:

```
MariaDB [course_registry]> alter table students auto_increment = 4;
Query OK, 3 rows affected (0.20 sec)
Records: 3  Duplicates: 0  Warnings: 0
```

In the preceding example, we are setting the value of auto_increment to 4, and MariaDB handles value management for the student_id column from here on. Let's insert another student but this time let's not insert a value for the student_id column and see how MariaDB handles this case. The code is as shown in the following screenshot:

```
MariaDB [course_registry]> insert into students(first_name, last_name,
 address, city, state, zip_code, username, password) values("Patrick",
 "Smith", "911A Clopper Rd", "Gburg", "MD", "20078", "patrick.smith",
SHA1("patricksmith"));
Query OK, 1 row affected, 2 warnings (0.11 sec)
```

In the preceding example, we are adding another student with the name Patrick Smith. Let's perform a SELECT query to retrieve the student_id, first_name, last_name, and username fields as shown in the following screenshot:

```
MariaDB [course_registry]> select student_id, first_name,
    -> last_name, username from students;
+------------+------------+-----------+---------------+
| student_id | first_name | last_name | username      |
+------------+------------+-----------+---------------+
|          1 | John       | Doe       | john.doe      |
|          2 | Jane       | Dane      | jane.dane     |
|          3 | Richard    | Roe       | richard.roe   |
|          4 | Patrick    | Smith     | patrick.smith |
+------------+------------+-----------+---------------+
4 rows in set (0.00 sec)
```

In the preceding example, we are retrieving the student records that are in the `students` table, and we can notice that the last record has a `student_id` of 4. And from here on, any student record that is added would automatically get the next available number. We have made a lot of changes to the `students` table in this chapter. Let's take a look at how the table structure has changed, as shown in the following screenshot:

```
MariaDB [course_registry]> describe students;
+------------+--------------+------+-----+---------+----------------+
| Field      | Type         | Null | Key | Default | Extra          |
+------------+--------------+------+-----+---------+----------------+
| student_id | int(11)      | NO   | PRI | NULL    | auto_increment |
| first_name | varchar(60)  | YES  |     | NULL    |                |
| last_name  | varchar(60)  | YES  |     | NULL    |                |
| address    | varchar(255) | YES  |     | NULL    |                |
| city       | varchar(40)  | YES  |     | NULL    |                |
| state      | char(2)      | YES  |     | NULL    |                |
| zip_code   | char(5)      | YES  |     | NULL    |                |
| username   | varchar(45)  | NO   | UNI | NULL    |                |
| password   | varchar(40)  | NO   |     | NULL    |                |
+------------+--------------+------+-----+---------+----------------+
9 rows in set (0.00 sec)
```

From the preceding result, we can notice all the changes that we have made; the first change is the new columns: `username` and `password`. The other changes include the unique key on the `username` column and the primary key on the `student_id` column. Also, notice that the `student_id` column will not take null values and will auto-increment the value upon each insert. Most of the SQL statements that we have worked on until now are simple statements that access one or multiple tables, most of which can throw SQL errors unless they are handled. When complex operations that require multiple SQL statements are performed, we can either run each of these statements one by one, or create a single unit that runs all these SQL statements in a specified order. One method of creating a single unit of multiple SQL statements is to use a **stored procedure**.

 Stored procedures build a cache based on the connection that is being established, which makes it tricky when used in the client-server architecture. We will research a little more of this behavior in *Chapter 7, Caching*.

Working with stored procedures

Using a stored procedure, we can wrap multiple SQL statements into a single unit that provides the integrity and consistency in which the SQL statements are executed. Assume that there are multiple developers performing the same set of tasks again and again, executing the same set of statements one at a time, in the same or a different order based on the developer's preferences. The process can be consolidated by putting these statements into a stored procedure. This single unit can be thoroughly tested for maintaining data integrity and executing consistency across different scenarios. Another reason why the stored procedures are preferred over a set of multiple SQL statements is the performance boost that the stored procedures provide. To build a stored procedure, we would need two things at a minimum, the first being the name of the stored procedure and the second being the body or the content inside the stored procedure. Let's write a simple stored procedure that would print out Hello World!. MariaDB solely depends on the statement delimiter (;) on when to execute the statements; since we will be dealing with multiple SQL statements with a stored procedure, we will temporarily switch the delimiter to something different, create a stored procedure, and then revert back to the default delimiter, as shown in the following screenshot:

```
-- Change the default delimiter
delimiter $$

create procedure p_helloWorld()
begin
        select "Hello World!";
end$$

-- Reset the delimiter
delimiter ;
```

In the preceding example, we begin by changing the statement delimiter from ; to $$; use the CREATE PROCEDURE DDL statement, and provide the name of the stored procedure. The name of the stored procedure is followed by (); any parameters for a stored procedure will be placed in these parentheses. We have to use these parentheses while declaring or calling a stored procedure irrespective of any parameters for the stored procedure.

 We will be using the "p_procedureName" convention for our stored procedures.

The content of a stored procedure is placed in between the BEGIN and END statements. These statements are used to scope the beginning and the end of the SQL statements for a stored procedure. Once the stored procedure has been defined, we will use the temporary delimiter to let MariaDB know that the stored procedure definition is ready for compilation. Once the stored procedure has been compiled, we reset the delimiter back to ;. We have successfully created our first stored procedure and now is the time to execute it and verify the output. To execute a stored procedure, we will use the CALL keyword, append it with the name of the stored procedure, and pass parameters to the stored procedure, if any are required. When we call our p_helloWorld() procedure, we should receive Hello World! as the output on the screen, as shown in the following screenshot:

```
MariaDB [course_registry]> call p_helloWorld();
+--------------+
| Hello World! |
+--------------+
| Hello World! |
+--------------+
1 row in set (0.00 sec)

Query OK, 0 rows affected (0.00 sec)
```

As we can see in the preceding example, we are successfully receiving the Hello World! output upon execution of the p_helloWorld() procedure. Working with stored procedures using MariaDB on the command line can get tricky sometimes, so we have to be very careful while creating and executing the stored procedures. Now that we have successfully created and executed a simple stored procedure, let's move on to a slightly more complex example where we will create a stored procedure that will take the first name, last name, address, city, state, zip code, username, and password as input parameters. The stored procedure would be intelligent enough to check the students table to see if there are any students with a similar username; if there are any, it would alert the user. If not, the procedure would use these input parameters to create a new student record.

The code is as shown in the following screenshot:

```
delimiter $$
create procedure p_insertStudents(
            IN pa_first_name varchar(60), IN pa_last_name varchar(60),
            IN pa_address varchar(255), IN pa_city varchar(40),
            IN pa_state char(2), IN pa_zip_code char(5),
            IN pa_username varchar(45), IN pa_password varchar(60)
        )
begin
            -- variable to hold the number of instances of this username
            declare ct_username int default 0;

            -- get the count and store it in ct_username
            select count(username) into ct_username from students where username=pa_username;

            -- check if username does not exist, if not, add the student
            if ct_username < 1 then
                    insert into students(first_name, last_name,
                                    address, city, state, zip_code,
                                    username, password
                        ) values(pa_first_name, pa_last_name,
                                    pa_address, pa_city,pa_state, pa_zip_code,
                                    pa_username, SHA1(pa_password)
                        );
                    select "Student has been successfully added!";
            else -- Alert the user
                    select "username already exists!";
            end if;

end$$
delimiter ;
```

We will be looking at four new concepts using this stored procedure: the first is the concept of defining multiple input parameters that are expected to be passed in by the user, the second will be declaring a variable inside a stored procedure, the third will be to store data into that variable, and the fourth concept will be to work with conditionals based on the value of the variable.

Consider the code in the following screenshot:

```
create procedure p_insertStudents(
            IN pa_first_name varchar(60), IN pa_last_name varchar(60),
            IN pa_address varchar(255), IN pa_city varchar(40),
            IN pa_state char(2), IN pa_zip_code char(5),
            IN pa_username varchar(45), IN pa_password varchar(60)
        )
```

In the preceding code, we are defining our procedure by giving the name of the stored procedure. This stored procedure accepts eight input parameters that will be used to create a new student's record.

 We will be using the "pa_columnname" convention for our input parameters.

The next snippet of code will deal with the creation of a variable inside a stored procedure. We will use the DECLARE keyword to create a procedure variable called ct_username that will keep a track of the count; that is, the number of times a username has been stored in the students table. As our variable will keep a track of the count, we will declare the datatype for this variable as an integer. As we are under the assumption that a new student is being added to our students table, we will default the value of ct_username to 0, as shown in the following screenshot:

```
-- variable to hold the number of instances of this username
declare ct_username int default 0;
```

Once we have declared the variable, the next step will be to retrieve the number of times the username that is being passed in via pa_username has been used in the students table, and store that username in the ct_username variable as shown in the following screenshot:

```
-- get the count and store it in ct_username
select count(username) into ct_username from students where username=pa_username;
```

Now that we have the count of the username that is being passed in as a parameter, we can use the count in the ct_username variable for making an informed decision; either to create a new record and give the user a success message or, if the username already exists, send an alert message back to the user. To perform this conditional check, we will be using the IF THEN, ELSE, and ENDIF constructs. We will begin by passing in a condition to the IF statement and use the THEN statement to indicate that when this condition is true, the block of SQL statements pertaining to the success case have to be executed.

We can also have an optional ELSE block to handle a situation where the IF condition is false as shown in the following screenshot:

```
-- check if username does not exist, if not, add the student
if ct_username < 1 then
        insert into students(first_name, last_name,
                        address, city, state, zip_code,
                        username, password
                ) values(pa_first_name, pa_last_name,
                        pa_address, pa_city,pa_state, pa_zip_code,
                        pa_username, SHA1(pa_password)
                );
        select "Student has been successfully added!";
else -- Alert the user
        select "username already exists!";
end if;
```

In the preceding code snippet, we are using the ct_username variable that has been populated in the previous step, and are making sure that there are no occurrences of that username. If the count that is returned is less than one (that is, zero), then SQL syntax in the IF block is executed and a new student record is created. If the count that is returned is not less than one (equal to or greater than one), the SQL statements in the ELSE block are executed, and the message is displayed onto the console. Let's take a look at the output when we call this stored procedure and provide the new student's information as shown in the following screenshot:

```
MariaDB [course_registry]> call p_insertStudents("William", "Dice",
    -> "779 Lebanon Rd.", "Frisco", "TX", "75034",
    -> "william.dice", "williamdice");
+---------------------------------------+
| Student has been successfully added! |
+---------------------------------------+
| Student has been successfully added! |
+---------------------------------------+
1 row in set (0.05 sec)

Query OK, 0 rows affected (0.05 sec)
```

As seen in the preceding screenshot, we get a success message saying Student has been successfully added. Now try and run the same call again and this time it will fail, as there is already a student record with the user william.dice. Whenever a new record is added to the students table, the AUTO INCREMENT functionality increments student_id, which is the primary key, by one. Now we know that student_id for William Dice will be 5, because there were four students ahead of him. However, when we are dealing with bulk imports, it will become very hard to manually keep a track of the last student's ID that was added. MariaDB provides a last_insert_id() function, using which we can retrieve the last successfully inserted ID for an AUTO INCREMENT column.

 Use select last_insert_id(); to print the last inserted ID.

In order to add this to our p_insertStudents() stored procedure, we will have to drop the existing stored procedure and create a new one with the updated code. Though MariaDB provides the ALTER PROCEDURE functionality, we can modify any characteristics of the procedure such as the definer or comment, but we cannot modify the parameters or the body of the stored procedure. Assuming we have all the required permissions, let's drop the procedure and rebuild the whole procedure again as shown in the following screenshot:

```
MariaDB [course_registry]> drop procedure p_insertStudents;
Query OK, 0 rows affected (0.00 sec)
```

 It is recommended to use DROP PROCEDURE IF EXISTS p_procedureName; to avoid an error if the procedure does not exist.

Now, let's make the required changes to the previous p_insertStudents procedure to add an extra parameter that would send the value of the last inserted ID out of the stored procedure. We will use the OUT keyword prepended to the parameter to denote that data will be retrieved out of the procedure using this new parameter as shown in the following screenshot:

```
delimiter $$
create procedure p_insertStudents(
                IN pa_first_name varchar(60), IN pa_last_name varchar(60),
                IN pa_address varchar(255), IN pa_city varchar(40),
                IN pa_state char(2), IN pa_zip_code char(5),
                IN pa_username varchar(45), IN pa_password varchar(60),
                OUT pa_student_id int
        )
begin
        -- variable to hold the number of instances of this username
        declare ct_username int default 0;

        -- get the count and store it in ct_username
        select count(username) into ct_username from students where username=pa_username;

        -- check if username does not exist, if not, add the student
        if ct_username < 1 then
                insert into students(first_name, last_name,
                                address, city, state, zip_code,
                                username, password
                        ) values(pa_first_name, pa_last_name,
                                pa_address, pa_city,pa_state, pa_zip_code,
                                pa_username, SHA1(pa_password)
                        );
                select "Student has been successfully added!";
                select last_insert_id() into pa_student_id;
        else -- Alert the user
                select "username already exists!";
        end if;

end$$
delimiter ;
```

There are two changes that have been made to the previous p_insertStudents procedure. Let's examine both carefully shown as follows:

```
create procedure p_insertStudents(
  IN pa_first_name varchar(60), IN pa_last_name varchar(60),
  IN pa_address varchar(255), IN pa_city varchar(40),
  IN pa_state char(2), IN pa_zip_code char(5),
  IN pa_username varchar(45), IN pa_password varchar(60),
  OUT pa_student_id int -- new parameter to send the id out
)
```

The first addition to the procedure is the new OUT parameter of datatype INT. This parameter will be used to send the last inserted ID out of the stored procedure shown as follows:

```
-- retrieve the last inserted id store it into the OUT parameter
select last_insert_id() into pa_student_id;
```

The second change that we have made is to store the last inserted ID into our OUT parameter, which is pa_student_id. Now let's create this procedure and call it as shown in the following screenshot:

```
MariaDB [course_registry]> call p_insertStudents("James", "Price",
    -> "11900 Hobby course ct.", "Austin", "TX", "78757",
    -> "james.price", "jamesprice", @student_id);
+---------------------------------------+
| Student has been successfully added!  |
+---------------------------------------+
| Student has been successfully added!  |
+---------------------------------------+
1 row in set (0.01 sec)

Query OK, 1 row affected (0.01 sec)

MariaDB [course_registry]> select @student_id;
+-------------+
| @student_id |
+-------------+
|           6 |
+-------------+
1 row in set (0.00 sec)
```

When working with OUT parameters, we will be using variables that are outside the stored procedure and are only passed into the stored procedure to retrieve the data. Session variables begin with a @ symbol unlike procedure variables that are declared inside stored procedures. While calling the stored procedure, we are giving the required information about the user and then using the @student_id session variable to retrieve the student's ID from our stored procedure. Commonly, we would need to declare the session variable and assign a datatype to that variable but since this will be used as an OUT parameter, the characteristics such as the datatype are applied by the stored procedure itself. Once the procedure is executed successfully, the value is stored in the @student_id variable. We will run the SELECT command to retrieve the value from this session variable.

The third type of parameter that can be used with stored procedures is the INOUT parameter where the parameter that carries that data can also carry out the modified data.

Working with stored routines

Stored routines are similar to stored procedures; both of them contain a block of SQL statements. There are a few differences such as a stored routine cannot return a result set and that a stored routine has to return a value and therefore, not preferred over stored procedures. Stored routines are invoked using the SELECT statement and can interchangeably be called as functions. The SHA1 function that we are using is a system-built stored routine to generate hashes for strings. Let's build a simple stored routine that would return the full name of the student when a username is passed in as a parameter, as shown in the following screenshot:

```
delimiter $$

create function fn_getFullName(pa_username varchar(45))
returns varchar(120) deterministic

begin

  declare fullname varchar(120) default "User does not exist";

  select concat(first_name, " ",last_name) into fullname
      from students where username=pa_username;

  return fullname;

end$$


delimiter ;
```

 We will be using the fn_functionName convention for our stored routines.

We begin by using the CREATE FUNCTION DDL command, appended by the name of the function, to create the function. This function takes the student's username as a parameter and returns the full name of the student, if the student exists. In the function, we begin by declaring a function variable called FullName, defaulted to the User does not exist message, which would be used if no student record is found. If the student record is found, we would retrieve the first name and last name of the student and use the CONCAT function that is provided by MariaDB to concatenate multiple strings. We are using the return keyword to return the data back, when the function is invoked. Let's invoke the function and pass a username that exists in the students table shown as follows:

```
MariaDB [course_registry]> select fn_getFullName("john.doe");
+---------------------------+
| fn_getFullName("john.doe") |
+---------------------------+
| John Doe                  |
+---------------------------+
1 row in set (0.00 sec)
```

In the preceding example, we are passing in the username of john.doe who is a valid student. Upon execution, we retrieve the valid full name of the student; that is, John Doe. Now, let's test a failure case where we pass in a username that does not exist in the students table as shown in the following screenshot:

```
MariaDB [course_registry]> select fn_getFullName("john.do");
+--------------------------+
| fn_getFullName("john.do") |
+--------------------------+
| User does not exist      |
+--------------------------+
1 row in set, 1 warning (0.00 sec)
```

In the preceding example, we have deleted the last character from the original username of John Doe. Upon execution, we get the default message that says User does not exist, which is true. The final example that we will work with in the stored routines is to drop the stored routine as shown in the following screenshot:

```
MariaDB [course_registry]> drop function fn_getFullName;
Query OK, 0 rows affected (0.00 sec)
```

We are using the DROP FUNCTION command to drop a stored routine.

 It is recommended to use DROP FUNCTION IF EXISTS fn_functionName; to avoid an error if the function does not exist.

Working with triggers

In the last few sections, we have looked at different scenarios for adding, updating, and deleting data. These are considered to be common operations in an everyday environment. However, what if we would like to watch certain events and use these events to perform another operation? As in, have an audit table that keeps a track of the user on whom an operation was performed or, assuming that there is a limit on the number of students that can register for a course, subtract that number whenever a student registers for the course. In our case, let's take a look at how an audit table can be used to keep track of different operations on a user. MariaDB provides the TRIGGER statement, which is a chain reaction that is set off in response to a SQL DML operation such as INSERT, UPDATE, or DELETE. To track these changes, let's build an audit table that would hold the person who performed the operation, the time when the operation was made, the type of the operation (INSERT, UPDATE, or DELETE), and the username on which the operation was performed, as shown in the following screenshot:

```
MariaDB [course_registry]> create table audit_students(
    ->          audit_id int not null auto_increment,
    ->          changed_by varchar(30),
    ->          changed_at datetime,
    ->          type char(1),
    ->          username varchar(45),
    ->          primary key(audit_id)
    -> );
Query OK, 0 rows affected (0.11 sec)
```

We will use the audit_students table to house the information about all the operations that are made on the students table. We will begin by creating a trigger that would track the INSERT operations on the students table.

For successfully creating a trigger, we would need at least four pieces of information; the first is the name of the trigger, which has to be unique; the second is the table with which the trigger will be associated; the third is the operation that fires our trigger; and the fourth is if the trigger is fired before or after the operation shown as follows:

```
delimiter $$

create trigger ti_students after insert on students
for each row
begin

    insert into audit_student(changed_by, changed_at, type, username)
        values(USER(), NOW(), "I",NEW.username);

end$$

delimiter ;
```

 We will be using the `ti_triggerName` convention for our triggers that will be fired upon inserts.

To create a trigger, we will use the CREATE TRIGGER DDL statement and append this with the name of the trigger. After we give the name for our trigger, we are mentioning when the trigger will be fired, which is *after* INSERT has been made on the students table. On the next row, we let MariaDB know how often the trigger should be fired, and will be fired on every row, shown as follows:

```
create trigger ti_students after insert on students
for each row
```

After this comes the body of the trigger where we will be keeping track of the SQL user who performed this operation, the time of the operation, the kind of operation, and finally the student on whom the operation was performed. Similar to a stored procedure and a stored routine, the body of the trigger will be inside the BEGIN and END statements, shown as follows:

```
begin

    insert into audit_students(changed_by, changed_at, type, username)
        values(USER(), NOW(), "I",NEW.username);

end$$
```

Inside the body of the trigger, we are performing an INSERT statement that would store the information about this operation, and we are storing that information in the audit_students table. The changed_by column tracks the SQL user that has performed this operation. There can be multiple users who have access to login into the MariaDB system and who are performing different operations based on their access rights. MariaDB provides the USER() function to retrieve the person who is currently performing the operation. Let's take a quick look at how this function can be used, shown as follows:

```
MariaDB [course_registry]> select user();
+----------------+
| user()         |
+----------------+
| root@localhost |
+----------------+
1 row in set (0.00 sec)
```

Now that we know who the SQL user is on MariaDB that is performing this operation, we will have to retrieve the time when this operation took place. The changed_at column tracks the time when this operation was performed, MariaDB provides the NOW() function to retrieve when this operation was made, shown as follows:

```
MariaDB [course_registry]> select now();
+---------------------+
| now()               |
+---------------------+
| 2014-02-01 00:48:43 |
+---------------------+
1 row in set (0.00 sec)
```

Now that we have the user and the time when this operation was made, we will use the letter I to denote that the operation that was made was an INSERT operation. MariaDB stores a copy of old or existing data in an alias called OLD and the new data in another alias called NEW. Since this is an INSERT operation, there will not be any data in OLD, but NEW will carry the student record that has just been added. We can use the dot (.) notation to access the data from NEW, so it will be NEW.columnname.

 We will use single-letter abbreviations for the operations that we are making: I for inserts, U for updates, and D for deletes.

Upon successful creation of the trigger, let's test this trigger by inserting a record into the students table, shown as follows:

```
MariaDB [course_registry]> select * from audit_students;
Empty set (0.00 sec)

MariaDB [course_registry]> insert into students(first_name, last_name, address,
city, state, zip_code, username, password) values("Robert","Senna","123 E. 10th
St","Omaha", "NE", "68107", "robert.senna", SHA1("robertsenna"));
Query OK, 1 row affected, 2 warnings (0.06 sec)

MariaDB [course_registry]> select * from audit_students;
+----------+---------------+---------------------+------+--------------+
| audit_id | changed_by    | changed_at          | type | username     |
+----------+---------------+---------------------+------+--------------+
|        1 | root@localhost | 2014-05-18 00:59:21 | I    | robert.senna |
+----------+---------------+---------------------+------+--------------+
1 row in set (0.00 sec)
```

We begin by testing if the audit_students table is empty and then use the INSERT statement to add a new student record with robert.senna as the username. Once the INSERT statement has been successfully executed, let's query the audit_students table to see if our trigger was fired after INSERT. Upon querying the audit_students table, we can see that a record was added after the user was added to the students table. Now, let's move on to the trigger that will be fired when an UPDATE statement is executed upon a record on the students table, shown as follows:

```
delimiter $$

create trigger tu_students after update on students
for each row
begin

    insert into audit_student(changed_by, changed_at, type, username)
        values(USER(), NOW(), "U",NEW.username);

end$$

delimiter ;
```

 We will be using the tu_triggerName convention for our triggers that will be fired upon updates.

This trigger is similar to the earlier trigger; we begin by using the CREATE TRIGGER DDL statement. As part of the creation, we are expecting this trigger to run after a successful update on the students table. This trigger contains the same query as the insert trigger because we are only looking for the username on whom the update has been performed.

 It is recommended to store complete record information, as it is hard to identify the exact column upon which the update was performed.

Once the trigger has been successfully created, let us make an update to the students table and see if our trigger is fired upon the update, shown as follows:

```
MariaDB [course_registry]> update students set address="123 E 10th St."
    -> where first_name = "Robert";
Query OK, 1 row affected, 2 warnings (0.11 sec)
Rows matched: 1  Changed: 1  Warnings: 2

MariaDB [course_registry]> select * from audit_students;
+----------+----------------+---------------------+------+--------------+
| audit_id | changed_by     | changed_at          | type | username     |
+----------+----------------+---------------------+------+--------------+
|        1 | root@localhost | 2014-02-01 01:24:53 | I    | robert.senna |
|        2 | root@localhost | 2014-02-01 01:27:33 | U    | robert.senna |
+----------+----------------+---------------------+------+--------------+
2 rows in set (0.00 sec)
```

In the preceding example, we are performing an update on the record that has a first_name as Robert. As we only have a single record with first_name as Robert, this would only update one record. Upon updating Robert's address, we have queried the audit_students table and the second record carries the information about the user who made the update, when this update was made, and on what record was the update made.

 It is always recommended to use the WHERE condition with a column that has been indexed; in our case, either student_id, which is the primary key or the username, which has a unique index. The first_name column has only been used for descriptive purposes, as this can cause multiple updates if there is more than one student with Robert as their first name.

Now, let's look at our last example that would be the trigger that is fired upon deletion of a student record, shown as follows:

```
delimiter $$

create trigger td_students before delete on students
for each row
begin

    insert into audit_students(changed_by, changed_at, type, username)
        values(USER(), NOW(), "D",OLD.username);

end$$

delimiter ;
```

 We will be using the td_triggerName convention for our triggers that will be fired upon deletes.

In the preceding example, we are creating a trigger that will be fired before a student record is deleted. This trigger is similar to the earlier triggers; the big difference is that this trigger will be fired when a student record is deleted. The other difference is that the single letter abbreviation is D to denote deletion; since a student record will not exist after the delete, the NEW alias here will be empty and we use the OLD alias to retrieve the required information.

 Triggers that are fired on UPDATE statements will have both NEW and OLD aliases populated.

Now the trigger has been successfully created, let's delete a record from the students table and see if our trigger is fired upon the delete, shown as follows:

```
MariaDB [course_registry]> delete from students where first_name="Robert";
Query OK, 1 row affected, 2 warnings (0.04 sec)

MariaDB [course_registry]> select * from audit_students;
+----------+---------------+---------------------+------+--------------+
| audit_id | changed_by    | changed_at          | type | username     |
+----------+---------------+---------------------+------+--------------+
|        1 | root@localhost | 2014-02-01 01:24:53 | I    | robert.senna |
|        2 | root@localhost | 2014-02-01 01:27:33 | U    | robert.senna |
|        3 | root@localhost | 2014-02-01 01:30:00 | D    | robert.senna |
+----------+---------------+---------------------+------+--------------+
3 rows in set (0.00 sec)
```

In the preceding example, we are deleting the student record with first_name as Robert. Upon successful deletion of this record, let's query the audit_students table; we can see that a third record is added having type as D that denotes deletion of a record, and the record that has been deleted has a username of robert.senna. The final example that we will work with is to drop the trigger. We will use the DROP TRIGGER DDL command to drop a trigger, shown as follows:

```
MariaDB [course_registry]> drop trigger td_students;
Query OK, 0 rows affected (0.06 sec)
```

Summary

In this chapter, we have covered a lot of advanced concepts such as altering tables, working with indexes and column characteristics, working with stored procedures, working with stored routines, and working with triggers. MariaDB offers many more advanced concepts and the concepts discussed in this chapter will lay a good foundation to acquire a better understanding of the more advanced database concepts. Now that we have talked about a few advanced concepts of MariaDB, let's switch gears and dive in to understand a popular programming paradigm called object-oriented programming and understand its implementation in PHP 5.

Advanced Programming with PHP

The most recognized minor version of PHP 5, in the last few years, is PHP 5.3, which has been widely accepted and is used currently. After PHP 5.3, two other minor versions of PHP, PHP 5.4, and PHP 5.5, have been released. Though a lot of hosting providers are still sticking with PHP 5.3, a few providers have started updating their PHP version to PHP 5.4. For users who do not depend on hosting providers, we can use the current version of PHP, PHP 5.5. There are a vast number of resources in books and on the Internet discussing the features of PHP 5.2 and 5.3, and very few resources discussing PHP 5.4 and 5.5. We will begin this chapter by learning a few new features that have been shipped out with PHP 5.4 and PHP 5.5.

 For more information about the object-oriented programming with PHP, please refer to the *Bonus chapter 2, Object-oriented Programming with PHP*.

New features in PHP 5.4 and 5.5

A lot of new features have been added to PHP with PHP 5.4 and 5.5. Most of these features were originally part of the PHP 6.0 release, which had to be postponed as rewriting PHP to support Unicode did not go as planned. Unicode is an industry standard character encoding set that supports most of the world languages, unlike ASCII that only encodes the Latin alphabet. One prominent issue that the developers faced during rewriting languages for Unicode support was that it almost took twice the runtime memory to execute the scripts. A few new features that have been shipped with PHP 5.4 and 5.5 are the ability to monitor upload progress, multiple improvements to arrays, a built-in web server, the password hashing API, the generators, partial Unicode support, updates to closures, and the powerful traits. PHP 5.4 and 5.5 arrives with multiple updates that will help us execute scripts faster and use less memory.

Updated array declaration

Short array syntax has been added to PHP 5.4 and we can now use the square brackets to declare arrays. Prior to this we would have had to use the array() language construct to declare and add elements to the array.

The following code is available in the array-declaration.php file, present in the code bundle:

```php
<?php

/**
 * Array declaration before PHP 5.4
 *
 */

$arr = array(1,2,3,4);

//Print an element to the screen
echo $arr[0]."\n";

/**
 * Array declaration with PHP 5.4 or greater
 *
 */

$arr2 = [1,2,3,4];

//Print an element to the screen
echo $arr2[0]."\n";

?>
```

In this example, we begin by looking at how an array declaration is done in the versions before PHP 5.4. We use the array() language construct and supply the array elements as arguments. In the second snippet, we are using the square brackets or the short syntax that has been shipped with PHP 5.4 to create an array. This syntax has been available in other scripting languages for a good amount of time, and this is a welcome addition to PHP. Let us execute this script and examine the output.

The output is of the previous code snippet is as follows:

```
1
1
```

Both the snippets print the first element of the array. If this script was executed with PHP 5.3, we would get a parse error as the engine encounters an unexpected square bracket.

The array dereferencing function

Array dereferencing has been added to PHP in PHP 5.4. Let us utilize this feature for retrieving elements from arrays that are returned by functions and/or methods. Prior to PHP 5.4, we would have had to store the array that is being returned by a function into a local variable before accessing an element. The following code is available in the `array-dereferencing.php` file, present in the code bundle:

```php
<?php

/**
 * Return an array of numbers
 *
 */

function retArray(){

        return ['a', 'b', 'c', 'd'];

}



/*
 * Before PHP 5.4
 * Assign data to a variable
 *
 */

$arr = retArray();
echo $arr[0]."\n";

/*
 * With PHP 5.4 or greater
 * Use the
 *
 */

echo retArray()[0]."\n";

?>
```

In this example, we begin by defining the `retArray()` function. This function returns an array of letters when invoked. The first snippet shows how the first element can be retrieved if we are using a PHP version prior to 5.4. In the second snippet, as array dereferencing for functions has been added in PHP 5.4, we can directly retrieve the element in a single step. Let us execute this script and examine the output.

The output of the previous code snippet is as follows:

```
a
a
```

The list() function in the foreach statement

One of the most common statements used to loop over an array of elements is the `foreach` statement. Prior to PHP 5.5, unpacking a nested array would have had to be done manually by referencing the index of that element. An interesting addition to PHP 5.5 is the ability to use the `list()` function to break a nested array into local variables in a `foreach` statement. Before we take a look at how the `list()` function and the `foreach` statement can be used together, let us get a quick refresher as to how the `list()` function works.

The following code is available in the `list.php` file, present in the code bundle:

```php
<?php
/*
 * Explanation of how list() works
 *
 */

list($one, $two, $three) = [1, 2, 3];
echo $one.' '.$two.' '.$three."\n";

?>
```

The `list()` function is a language construct used to assign a list of variables in a single operation. In this example, we begin by assigning an array of numbers to a list of variables using the `list()` languages construct. In the next step, we are echoing these variables to the screen.

The output of the previous code snippet is as follows:

```
1 2 3
```

The `list()` language construct has been around since PHP 4; with PHP 5.5, we can use it with the `foreach` statement.

The following code is available in the `foreachlist.php` file, present in the code bundle:

```php
<?php
/**
 * A list of students
 */
$students = [
            [
                    "John",
                    "Doe",
                    101
            ],
            [
                    "Jane",
                    "Dane",
                    102
            ],
        ];

//Print student data without list()
foreach($students as $student){

        echo $student[0].' '.$student[1].' '.$student[2]."\n";

}

//Print student data using list()
foreach($students as list($first_name, $last_name, $student_id)){

        echo $first_name.' '.$last_name.' '.$student_id."\n";

}

?>
```

In this example, we begin by creating a list of students; each student is a list of attributes such as the first name, last name, and age. In the first snippet, we are not using the `list()` construct, so we will have to pick each element from every student by the index. With PHP 5.5, we can now use the `list()` construct with the `foreach` statement to directly load the values into temporary variables. When we execute this script, the output will be the same for both of the snippets; the main difference here is that the second snippet is easier on the eyes as we are dealing with variable names that represent the data stored in that variable. Let us execute this script and examine the output.

The output of the previous code snippet is as follows:

```
John Doe 101
Jane Dane 102
John Doe 101
Jane Dane 102
```

As expected, the output of both the snippets is the same.

Availability of $this in closures

Until PHP 5.4, when closures were declared in a class, they would have been considered as anonymous functions that would not have access to the surrounding properties and methods. With PHP 5.4, the anonymous functions will behave as closures where they will have access to the surrounding properties and methods via the $this instance variable.

The following code is available in the closures.php file, present in the code bundle:

```php
<?php
/*
* Student class
*
*/
class Student{
        private $name = "John Doe";

        function getName(){
                return function(){

                        //$this is not available
                        //inside closures
                        return $this->name;
                };
        }

}

$student = new Student();
$name = $student->getName();

echo $name()."\n";

?>
```

In this example, we are creating a closure to return the value of the $name property. Prior to PHP 5.4, though closures existed, they did not have access to the $this instance variable. Let us execute this script and examine the output.

The output of the previous code snippet is as follows:

```
John Doe
```

Class member access on instantiation

The next feature that we will be looking at is the ability to access members of a class upon instantiation. For this example, we will work with the range(), rand(), min(), and max() functions. The range() function takes a minimum of two values as parameters to return an array of elements between those values. The rand() function returns a random number when the minimum and maximum limits are passed in. The min() and max() functions return the least and the maximum values in an array.

The following code is available in the classMemberAccess.php file, present in the code bundle:

```php
<?php

/*
 * Students class
 *
 */
class Students{
        private $studentIds;

        function __construct(){

                $this->studentIds = range(1, 500);

        }

        function getRandomStudent(){

                return rand(min($this->studentIds),
                  max($this->studentIds));

        }

}
```

```
//Before PHP 5.4
$student = new Students();
echo $student->getRandomStudent()."\n";


//Using PHP 5.4 or greater
echo (new Students())->getRandomStudent()."\n";

?>
```

In this example, we are creating a `Students` class. This class carries the `$studentIds` property that would store the ID of all the students. For this example, let us populate this property using the `range()` function. The aim of this script is to retrieve a random student and print his/her ID; we will be using the `getRandomStudent()` method to retrieve the random student's ID.

 We can extend this example to create a system that would assign a different set of question papers based on the picked student's ID. This will not be a part of this book, but readers are welcome to try this example.

In the first snippet, we are creating an instance of the `Students` class and are assigning it to a local variable. After that we use the local variable (an object of that class) to call the `getRandomStudent()` method. In the second snippet, we are creating an instance and then using that instance on-the-fly to call the `getRandonStudent()` method. Before PHP 5.4, this was a two-step process where we would create an instance and assign that to a local variable, and then use the local variable to call a method; however, with PHP 5.4, we can directly call the method in a single step.

The output for the previous code snippet is as follows:

```
332
224
```

As we are generating these student's IDs using the `rand()` function, the IDs are not the same.

Generators

A generator is very similar to a function that returns an array, the difference being (as the name suggests) that a generator generates a sequence of values. In PHP, we will have to implement the `Iterator` interface for object iteration, which can sometimes get a little tedious. A generator already implements the `Iterator` interface, so this reduces the complexity of building an iterator. The first difference between a function returning an array and a generator is that the generator uses the `yield` keyword.

The following code is available in the `student-generator.php` file, present in the code bundle:

```php
<?php

/*
 * Generator- yields a student at a time
 */
function students(){
        yield "John Doe";
        yield "Jane Dane";
        yield "Richard Roe";
}

foreach(students() as $student){

        echo $student."\n";
}

?>
```

In this example, we are yielding three students via the `student()` generator. Later, we are running our generator through the `foreach` construct to retrieve one student at a time. The difference between returning data via a function and yielding the data with a generator is that a generator will retain the state and yield the next value when it is used again. This behavior is unlike a function, where it would return the whole array upon invoking again. Let us execute the script and examine the output.

The output for the previous code snippet is as follows:

```
John Doe
Jane Dane
Richard Roe
```

Upon execution, the script will print the names of each student on the screen, but this looks similar to what we would do with a `return` statement. Generators are commonly used to perform tasks that apply to large datasets; an example would be a set of operations on a file that has over a million lines. If we would handle a file with so much data, a lot of memory would not only be dedicated to store the file in memory, but also the PHP arrays that would store that data. PHP arrays are very expensive as they are ordered HashMaps that provide on-demand access to data, making it resource-intensive. Ordered HashMaps are associative arrays, which are internally used to store data on the RAM. Let us now look at a real-time implementation of generators to handle the file operations.

 This example is just for demonstration purposes as providing a file that is over 800 MB is unrealistic.

The following code is available in the `file-reader.php` file, present in the code bundle:

```php
<?php

function fileData($fileName) {
        $file = fopen($fileName, 'r');

        while (($line = fgets($file)) !== false) {
                yield $line;
        }

        fclose($file);
}

foreach (fileData('bigData.csv') as $line) {
//file operations
}

?>
```

In this example, we are building a generator to return the data from a large file and then we perform our file operations one line at a time. By using generators, not only do we save memory but, as the data size gets larger, the execution time compared to other methods will be far shorter.

Traits

In *Bonus chapter 2, Object-oriented Programming with PHP*, we discussed object-oriented concepts in PHP and worked with inheritance to understand how functionality in one class can be extended to other classes and how common functionality can be shared among different subclasses. With PHP 5.4, we will go over a new concept called **Traits** that facilitates using the functionality from more than one source at a time. If we would have to achieve this prior to PHP 5.4, we would have ended up duplicating the code into multiple classes as required by making our code difficult to work with. This is commonly referred to as **horizontal inheritance**. To declare a trait, we will use the `trait` keyword followed by the name of the trait; the functionality for the trait will be placed inside the curly braces next to the trait.

The following code is available in the `trait.php` file, present in the code bundle:

```php
<?php

class BaseClass{

        public function helloWorld(){

                echo "Hello World from Base Class \n";

        }

}

trait MyTrait{

        public function helloWorldFromTrait(){

                echo "Hello World from Trait\n";

        }

}

class SubClass extends BaseClass{

        use MyTrait;

}
```

```
$obj = new SubClass();
$obj->helloWorld();
$obj->helloWorldFromTrait();


?>
```

In this example, we have two classes and a trait. The subclass is already extending the functionality of the base class. When a subclass would like to use the functionality of another entity other than its base class, we can house such reusable functionality in a trait and let the subclasses use the trait. To use the functionality from a trait, we will use the keyword use. Let us execute this script and examine the output.

The output of the previous code snippet is as follows:

```
Hello World from Base Class
Hello World from Trait
```

To use multiple traits, we will use the comma separator to add more than one trait to a class.

Here is an example of the syntax to be followed:

```
class SubClass extends BaseClass{

        use Trait1, Trait2, Trait3;

}
```

 This code is only for demonstration purpose and should not be executed by adding the required class and traits.

Traits are a very powerful feature and help us in making our code more reusable and object-oriented. A real-time implementation of traits is to create a singleton trait that can convert any class into a singleton when used. Given the numerous ways of working with traits, they will certainly be one of the popular additions to PHP 5.4.

Addition of the finally block to exception handling

In this section, we will take a quick look at exception handling and the addition of the `finally` block in PHP 5.5. Exception handling is commonly used to alter the flow of execution when a specified condition occurs. Exceptions can be caused due to different events such as a file not being available to be used, a faulty database connection, or just bad code. By using an exception handling strategy, we will be able to predict any exceptions that might occur and handle these exceptions in a graceful method. In PHP, the exceptions are thrown during the code execution and to catch these exceptions we will use the `try` block and add our code into the `try` block to catch the error. If the exception is not caught and handled, a fatal error will occur that will halt the execution of our script.

The following code is available in the `exceptionHandling.php` file, present in the code bundle:

```php
<?php

function divide($a, $b){

        try{
                if($b ==0){

                        throw new Exception("Divide by Zero
                          Exception");

                }

                return $a/$b;
        }
        catch(Exception $ex){

                //a good practice to log the exceptions
                return $ex->getMessage();

        }
}

echo divide(4,0)."\n";

?>
```

In this example, we begin by defining the `divide()` function that would take two integers as parameters and recreate the `Divide By Zero` exception. We will place the code that is performing the division into the `try` block. In our code, we are checking to see if the value of the second parameter that is being used as the denominator is equal to zero. If the condition is a success, we will throw a new exception and pass the message. The `catch` block that is placed right after the `try` block will catch this exception and return the exception message back to the execution.

The output of the previous code snippet is as follows:

```
Divide by Zero Exception
```

Until now we can either throw an exception or catch an exception; with PHP 5.5, we can use the `finally` block to handle any kind of closing operations. The `finally` block is executed after the `try` and `catch` blocks are executed. One common example is deleting any file resource links that were created during the `try` block. Another example is unlocking tables that have been locked or closing an open database connection.

The following code is available in the `exceptionHandlingWithFinally.php` file, present in the code bundle:

```php
<?php

function divide($a, $b){

        try{
                if($b ==0){
                        throw new Exception("Divide by Zero
                          Exception");
                }

                echo $a/$b."\n";
        }
        catch(Exception $ex){
                //a good practice to log the exceptions
                echo $ex->getMessage()."\n";
        }
        finally{
                //perform clean up operations
                echo "executed after try & catch \n";
        }
}

divide(4,0);

?>
```

We are continuing with the example that we used earlier, and have added the `finally` block that can be used to perform any sort of clean-up operations as required.

The output of the previous code snippet is as follows:

```
Divide by Zero Exception
executed after try & catch
```

The goal of exception handling is for our application to run without crashing or throwing errors. Although it is an ideal situation for the application to perform without crashing, exception handling helps us get our application closer to performing without crashing. All applications are built with a set of assumptions; so as long as the users proceed along an expected route, the application will perform as expected. And when a user performs an unexpected action, the PHP engine sends an unexpected response back. Exception handling helps us to handle such unexpected responses in a graceful manner. As good programmers, it is very important for us to predict and identify such cases.

Unit testing

Now that we understand exception handling, this is a good place to take a look at the concept of unit testing. As the name suggests, unit testing refers to testing the application one unit at a time. A unit is an arbitrary term but it is always advised to divide the code into the smallest independent working fragment and test that unit. In this section, we will briefly go over automated unit tests. Automated unit testing makes the process of testing the functionality easier as the application grows. Let us take the example of a student portal. We begin by building a simple portal that will allow us to add a student. Once we provide the portal to add students, the users of the portal would need an interface to view the student information that they have added. Once we provide this interface, they might request the development team for a lot more features. As we keep adding features, the amount of functionality that has to be tested will increase, and sometimes the code that has been added to support one functionality might either break or not coexist with the code of another functionality. Normally these issues are identified by regression testing, and automated unit testing helps the developers to understand and predict where a code fix might cause issues at another location. We will be using the **PHPUnit** testing framework, which is an instance of the **xUnit** architecture for unit-testing frameworks.

Installing PHPUnit

The installation process for PHPUnit is pretty simple and we will install PHPUnit v3.7, which was the stable version while writing this book. The installation commands will be same on all operating systems, as we will use the **PHP Extension and Application Repository (PEAR)** to get and install the PHPUnit libraries. PEAR is a distributed code repository that is used to maintain common code packages, and other developers and development teams can use the `pear` command to download them onto their local environments.

 These commands should be run in the terminal window on a Linux or Mac OS X operating system or in the command prompt window on the Windows operating system.

Here are the two lines of command we will need here:

```
pear config-set auto_discover 1
pear install pear.phpunit.de/PHPUnit
```

Using the first command we are setting up the configuration to allow PEAR to automatically discover new channels from the command line or to look for dependencies that are required while installing a library. With the second command, we are installing the PHPUnit framework, which also installs other dependencies such as the `File_Iterator` library, the `PHP_Timer` library, and the `PHP_CodeCoverage` library. Upon running these commands, the PHPUnit framework and its dependencies will be successfully installed. To verify the installation, we can run the `phpunit` command and add the option to print out the version of PHPUnit that we have installed. After this, the following code needs to be run:

```
phpunit --version
```

This has to be run using the same command-line utility that was used earlier to install the PHPUnit library.

The output for the previous command line is as follows:

```
PHPUnit 3.7.32 by Sebastian Bergmann.
```

Upon execution of the command, the version 3.7.32 will be printed onto the screen. Sebastian Bergmann is the creator of PHPUnit. Now that we have successfully installed PHPUnit, we are all set to write our first test.

The following code is available in the exampleTest.php file, present in the code bundle:

```php
<?php

class exampleTest extends PHPUnit_Framework_TestCase{

        public function testTrue(){

                $this->assertTrue(true);

        }

        public function testCount(){
                $array = [1,2,3,4];

                $this->assertCount(4, $array);

        }
}

?>
```

There are three important things to note from our test case (exampleTest.php):

- The test case will always inherit from PHPUnit_Framework_TestCase.
- The tests inside the test case will always be public and are named test*. We can also use the @test annotation in the method's doc block.
- As part of conventions, the name of the test case and the filename carrying the test should always end with test.

The tests inside a test case will carry an assert method that is used to ensure that the data that is being passed in matches the expected result. In our tests, we are looking at two different assert methods; the first assert method checks to see if the value being passed in is true, while the second assert method ensures that the array length is equal to the expected value that has been passed in.

 To run a test case, use the phpunit command that we have used earlier in phpunit exampleTest.php.

The output for the previous code snippet is as follows:

```
PHPUnit 3.7.32 by Sebastian Bergmann.


..


Time: 80 ms, Memory: 1.25Mb


OK (2 tests, 2 assertions)
```

We have successfully asserted both our tests; when the message says that there are two tests and two assertions, it means that both of our tests have been asserted or have passed. Now let us build a custom class with a single method and then come up with a test case that would have multiple tests focusing on that method. Just to verify the output message for a failed test, let us add a test that would fail.

The following code is available in the `Math.php` file, present in the code bundle:

```php
<?php

class Math{

        /**
        * returns the sum of two numbers
        **/
        function add($a, $b){

                return $a + $b;

        }

}

?>
```

This is a very basic class that has an `add()` method that takes two numbers as input and returns their sum. Now let us create a test case for the `Math` class.

The following code is available in the `MathTest.php` file, present in the code bundle:

```php
<?php
require_once('Math.php');

class MathTest extends PHPUnit_Framework_TestCase{
```

```php
    public function testAdd(){

        $this->assertEquals(5, (new Math())->add(2,3));

    }

    public function testAdd2(){

        $this->assertNotEquals(6, (new Math())->add(2,3));


    }

    public function testAdd3(){

        $this->assertEquals(4, (new Math())->add(2,3));

    }
}
?>
```

In this test case, we have three tests that are passing in numbers two and three to the add() method and are testing to see if the expected value matches with the result. The first two tests will be successful, as the first test is asserting to see if the value returned by the method is equal to five. Upon execution, this will be a successful test. The second test is asserting to see if the value returned by the method is not equal to six. Upon execution, this test will be successful too. In the last test, we are asserting if the value returned by the add() method is equal to four. This will fail as the value returned will be five.

The output of the previous code snippet is as follows:

```
PHPUnit 3.7.32 by Sebastian Bergmann.

..F

Time: 89 ms, Memory: 1.50Mb

There was 1 failure:

1) MathTest::testAdd3
Failed asserting that 5 matches expected 4.

/var/www/UnitTesting/MathTest.php:21

FAILURES!
Tests: 3, Assertions: 3, Failures: 1.
```

As expected, the last assertion failed while the other two were successful. Refactor the code to remove the last assertion and utilize the documentation available on the PHPUnit website to discover more about how to implement unit testing in your projects. Unit testing might appear to add more time in the development of a project or a feature. However, this will help in reducing the total time taken by us to manually test the whole application every time a new feature is added. PHPUnit also comes with multiple other features such as custom bootstrapping that would allow us autoload the required files rather than using `require` or `require_once`; another popular feature is code coverage that helps us find dead code. Dead code is code that still exists in our project but isn't being used. There are numerous features provided by PHPUnit and a good place to understand and read about these features is the official website of PHPUnit at `http://phpunit.de/manual/current/en/`.

Working with MariaDB

So far we have worked with core programming concepts of PHP and we have also worked with the MariaDB database server in *Chapter 1, CRUD Operations, Sorting, Filtering, and Joins* and *Chapter 2, Advanced Programming with MariaDB*. In this section, let us focus on setting up communication between PHP and MariaDB. PHP provides three APIs to connect to MariaDB; they are as follows:

API	Description	Comment
mysql	This is probably the most used API to connect to MySQL and MariaDB databases. This API has been around since PHP 2.0. Active development for this API has been stopped and it is not advised to use this API in any of new projects.	The mysql API has been deprecated since PHP 5.5.0 and will be removed in the future.
mysqli	MySQL Improved is the new API that has been introduced with PHP 5. This API is a huge upgrade over the last API. This API supports features such as client-side and server-side prepared statements, stored procedures, and transactions. This API has an object-oriented interface and a procedural interface.	The mysqli API stands for MySQL Improved.
PDO	PDO is an object-oriented interface to work with a database. PDO can support a wide range of databases as this provides the flexibility to move to other database management systems at some point in the future.	The PDO API stands for PHP Data Objects.

We will go over examples for both `mysqli` and `PDO` in this section and it is recommended to go over the API documentation provided at `http://www.php.net/manual/en/mysqlinfo.api.choosing.php` to make an informed decision.

PHP – mysqli

Though the `mysqli` API supports both procedural and OOP interfaces, we will use the OOP interface for this example. To work with this example, let us create an `employee` database with a few employee records.

The following code is available in the `employees.sql` file, present in the code bundle:

```
CREATE DATABASE IF NOT EXISTS `employee_db`;
--
-- Database: `employee_db`
--


-- --------------------------------------------------------


USE `employee_db`;
--
-- Table structure for table `employees`
--

CREATE TABLE IF NOT EXISTS `employees` (
  `id` int(11) NOT NULL AUTO_INCREMENT,
  `first_name` varchar(60) NOT NULL,
  `last_name` varchar(60) NOT NULL,
  PRIMARY KEY (`id`)
) ENGINE=InnoDB  DEFAULT CHARSET=latin1 AUTO_INCREMENT=4 ;


--
-- Dumping data for table `employees`
--

INSERT INTO `employees` (`id`, `first_name`, `last_name`) VALUES
(1, 'John', 'Doe'),
(2, 'Jane', 'Dane'),
(3, 'Richard', 'Roe');
```

Now that we have created the required data in the employee database, let's use the mysqli API to connect to the database and fetch the employee records.

The following code is available in the php-mysqli.php file, present in the code bundle:

```php
<?php

//store connection parameters in constants
define("DB_HOST","localhost");
define("DB_NAME","employee_db");
define("DB_USER","root");
define("DB_PASSWORD", "admin");

//establish a database connection
$connection = new mysqli(DB_HOST, DB_USER, DB_PASSWORD, DB_NAME);

if($connection->connect_error) {

  trigger_error("Database connection failed: "   . $conn->connect_error,
E_USER_ERROR);

}


//query to retrieve employees
$sql = "select id, first_name, last_name from employees;";

//execute the query
$result = $connection->query($sql);

//check if result is valid
if($result === false){

  trigger_error("Sql Error, verify SQL", E_USER_ERROR);

}

//iterate over the result
while($row = $result->fetch_assoc()){

  echo $row['id']." ".$row['first_name']." ".$row['last_name']."\n";

}

?>
```

In this example, we begin by storing the connection parameters to the database in the constants and then we create a `mysqli` object and use the connection parameters to establish a connection. In the next step, we verify if the connection was successful. If this isn't true, we will trigger an error so that appropriate steps can be taken. In the next step, we will query the database to retrieve the available employee records and then we will iterate over the retrieved record set to print the information about each employee.

The output for the previous code is as follows:

```
1 John Doe
2 Jane Dane
3 Richard Roe
```

PHP – PDO

In this section, we will use the PDO API to fetch all of the employee records from the employees table.

The following code is available in the `php-pdo.php` file, present in the code bundle:

```php
<?php

//store connection parameters in constants
define("DB_HOST","localhost");
define("DB_NAME","employee_db");
define("DB_USER","root");
define("DB_PASSWORD", "admin");

try{
        //establish a connection
        $connection = new
          PDO("mysql:host=".DB_HOST.";dbname=".DB_NAME, DB_USER,
          DB_PASSWORD);

        //set error mode
        $connection->setAttribute(PDO::ATTR_ERRMODE,
          PDO::ERRMODE_EXCEPTION);

        //query to retrieve employees
        $sql = "select id, first_name, last_name from employees";

        $data = $connection->query($sql);
        foreach($data as list($id, $first_name, $last_name)){
                echo $id." ".$first_name." ".$last_name."\n";
        }
```

```
}
catch(Exception $ex){
        echo $ex->getMessage();
}
finally{
        $connection = null;
}
?>
```

In the preceding example, we begin by building a PDO object. In the next step, we are setting the error reporting mode to ERRMODE_EXCEPTION. This will route the execution to the `catch` block and an exception of the class PDO_EXCEPTION is thrown. In the next step, we are executing our `select` query and we are printing the results out onto the screen.

The output for the previous code is as follows:

```
1  John Doe
2  Jane Dane
3  Richard Roe
```

Now that we have worked with both MariaDB and unit testing, this is a good place to set up a test case to test the database integrity. A few operations that we can perform are to create tables and insert data into those tables on-the-fly. Once we have the data in those tables, we can perform the `select` queries to verify if all the data has been inserted, or even verify if a specific row was inserted as part of a spot check. Once our tests are successful, we can drop the tables and continue with our development. Let us look at a very basic example for testing the data integrity.

The following code is available in the `DatabaseTest.php` file, present in the code bundle:

```php
<?php

class DatabaseResult extends PHPUnit_Framework_TestCase{

        private $connection;

        public function setUp(){
                //set up
                $this->connection = new
                    PDO("mysql:host=localhost;dbname=employee_db",
                    "root", "admin");

                $this->connection->setAttribute(PDO::ATTR_ERRMODE,
                    PDO::ERRMODE_EXCEPTION);
```

```
        }

        public function testData(){

                $data = $this->connection->query("select count(*)
                    as ct from employees where first_name =
                    'John';")->fetchObject();

                $this->assertEquals(1, $data->ct);

        }

        public function tearDown(){
                //clean up
                $this->connection = null;
        }
    }
?>
```

In this example, we begin by establishing a connection to the database in the setup() fixture, which is used to fetch the data during our test. We are using the setup() and tearDown() fixtures in our example; they are referred to as test fixtures in the xUnit architecture. A test fixture is defined as a point where everything that is required to successfully run a test has to be available. The setup() test fixture is commonly used to create the required resources, while the teardown() fixture would clean up all the resources that were set up. In our example, we are using the setup() fixture to establish a database connection, while we are ending that database connection in the tearDown() fixture.

The output of the previous code snippet is as follows:

```
PHPUnit 3.7.32 by Sebastian Bergmann.


.


Time: 91 ms, Memory: 1.50Mb

OK (1 test, 1 assertion)
```

Here we can see that our test was successful.

Summary

In this chapter, we have taken a look at a few new features that are available with PHP 5.4 and PHP 5.5. We have also looked at unit testing, and how it could help us streamline our software development life cycle by testing individual units of our application by using PHPUnit's test cases. The last topic that we have discussed is establishing a connection with our MariaDB database. In the next chapter, we will begin by discussing how HTML interacts with PHP and move forward with building our student portal application.

4

Setting Up Student Portal

In the previous chapter, we went over a few advanced concepts such as the new features that are part of PHP 5.4 and 5.5, using unit testing to test individual units of an application, and different methods of connecting to the MariaDB database server in order to retrieve data. In this chapter, we will use all the concepts that we have learned in the earlier chapters to build an application. Until now, we have used PHP CLI to execute most of the scripts that we have worked with. In this chapter, we will use PHP to build an interactive student portal. Using this student portal, we can perform the following tasks:

- Setting up the nuts and bolts of our application
- Setting up MVC
- Adding a student
- Listing all students
- Adding a course
- Listing all courses
- Registering a student to a course
- Viewing all registrations

We will use HTML, PHP, and MariaDB to accomplish these tasks.

Setting up the nuts and bolts of our application

In *Bonus chapter 2, Object-oriented Programming with PHP*, we discussed design patterns and how we can use design patterns to better organize our code. We will use the MVC design pattern to build our student portal application. The **MVC** pattern or the **Model-View-Controller** pattern is one of the most used patterns to build web applications. The features of MVC are as follows:

- The model is responsible for data management. The model handles the common data operations such as retrieving, updating, and deleting data.

- The view is responsible for data presentation. The view will commonly carry the required HTML that would be responsible for displaying the data on the browser.

- The controller is responsible for data processing. The controller houses any application logic that has to be performed on the data that has been retrieved by the model, before sending it to the view. A controller can have one or many actions that will serve as a single functional unit of the application logic. An action is a method in the controller.

In order to build a MVC-based web application, we will need to fulfill a few prerequisites such as activating the rewrite functionality on Apache, and setting up the directory structure for our application. We will need the rewrite functionality to implement clean URLs that are easier to read than a complicated query string.

Before using the rewrite functionality, the URL is as follows:

```
http://student-portal/index.php?url=students
```

After using the rewrite functionality, the URL changes to:

```
http://student-portal/students
```

Setting up URL rewrite

Apache web server is shipped with a number of very useful modules; one of them is the mod_rewrite module. The mod_rewrite module provides a rule-based engine to rewrite URLs on-the-fly. We can also use this module to redirect one URL to another URL and to invoke an internal proxy fetch. By using the mod_rewrite module, we can successfully hide the file system path from users.

The `mod_rewrite` module is turned off by default and has to be explicitly turned on. To turn on the `mod_rewrite` module, we will have to either modify the configuration files of the Apache web server in a few operating systems or use internal commands to turn on the module. In Ubuntu, we will use the `a2enmod` command to turn on the `mod_rewrite` module:

```
sudo a2enmod rewrite
```

As the `mod_rewrite` module is turned off by default, the overriding capability of Apache to override URLs dynamically is also turned off. To turn this back on, we will look for the `apache2.conf` file or the `httpd.conf` file, and search for the string `AllowOverride`. It will be set to `None` by default, and we will have to change it to `All`. This change has to be applied only to the document root that we are currently working with and not anything else, as this could create security issues:

```
Before
<Directory /var/www/>
  Options Indexes FollowSymLinks
  AllowOverride None
  Require all granted
</Directory>

After
<Directory /var/www/>
  Options Indexes FollowSymLinks
  AllowOverride all
  Require all granted
</Directory>
```

As we have made the changes to core Apache configuration files, we will have to restart the Apache web server. To restart the web server, we will use the `restart` command:

```
sudo service apache2 restart
```

Now that we have added the rewrite functionality, let us go ahead and set up the folder structure that we will use for building our MVC student application. This script has to be run in a terminal window and has to be run in the document root folder. Now, we create a folder structure using the following commands, in the `build.sh` script:

```
mkdir student-portal
cd student-portal
mkdir models
mkdir controllers
mkdir views
mkdir lib
```

The `build.sh` script will create the required folder structure for housing our scripts. Let us begin by creating the `index.php` page that would serve as our entry point to our student portal. We will be using this `index.php` page as our primary landing point and router. To set this as our primary router, we will use the `.htaccess` file where we will put our web server rules and conditions.

 The `.htaccess` file is commonly used to decentralize the management of web server configurations. Using the `.htaccess` file, we will be able to add in application-specific web server configurations. The `.htaccess` file is housed in the directory of the application, and the configurations in this file override any global web server configurations.

In our `.htaccess` file, we will begin by turning on the rewrite engine that is available via the `mod_rewrite` module and route all the requests to our `index.php` page. During this routing process, we will extract the first part from the URL and redirect this call to our `index.php` with `url` query string parameter.

An example URL request that will be made is as follows:

```
localhost/student-portal/student
```

The redirected URL will be as follows:

```
localhost/student-portal/index.php?url=student
```

This redirect is done in order to capture the page that was requested and then process the request from there on. We will use an `.htaccess` file to facilitate the redirect that contains the following code:

```
RewriteEngine On

RewriteCond %{REQUEST_FILENAME} !-f
RewriteCond %{REQUEST_FILENAME} !-d
RewriteCond %{REQUEST_FILENAME} !-l

RewriteRule ^(.*)$ index.php?url=$1 [QSA,L]
```

This script should be added to the document's root directory and the file should be saved as `.htaccess`. Now let us add our `index.php` and verify if our application level web server configurations in the `.htaccess` script have been applied on request. Add the following code to the `index.php` file:

```php
<?php

$url = $_GET['url'];
echo '"'.$url.'"'.' is the requested page';

?>
```

In our `index.php` file, we are retrieving the value of `url` that will be populated during the redirection process.

The output is as follows:

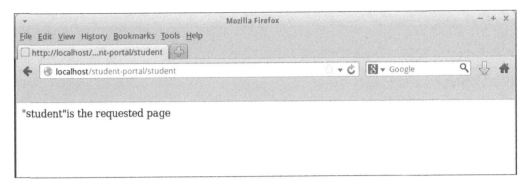

Since **"student" is the requested page** is printed, we can believe that our redirection was successful. Now let us continue with our student application and build our first form that will allow us to add a student to our `course_registry` database.

> We will be working with the `course_registry` database that we built in *Chapter 1, CRUD Operations, Sorting, Filtering and Joins on MariaDB*, and *Chapter 2, Advanced Programming with MariaDB*.

Setting up MVC

Now that we have our folder structure and the rewrite functionality working, we can begin setting up our MVC-based application. The first thing that we will have to focus on would be to bootstrap our application by loading the required classes. We are storing these required classes in the `lib` folder and we will use the `config.php` file to store the required configurations such as the location of the `lib` folder, the base URL for our application, and the database connection information.

```php
<?php
define('LIBRARY', 'lib/');
define('BASE_URL', 'http://localhost/student-portal/');

define('DB_VENDOR','mysql');
define('DB_HOST','localhost');
define('DB_NAME','course_registry');
define('DB_USR','root');
define('DB_PWD','top_secret_pwd');
```

Let us add the `Bootstrap` class in our `lib` folder. This class will be responsible for understanding, interpreting, and redirecting the incoming request to the correct controller. The code to be entered in `lib/Bootstrap.php` class is as follows:

```php
<?php
class Bootstrap{

  public function __construct(){

    $url = $_GET['url'];
    $url = explode("/",$url);

    //should be logged
    //if a controller is not mentioned
    if(empty($url[0])){
    require_once("controllers/students.php");
(new Students())->get();
    return false;
}
$file_name = "controllers/".$url[0].".php";

    //should be logged
    if(!file_exists($file_name)){
      //replace the message
      //redirect the user to a custom 404 page
      echo "File does not exist";
      return false;
}

    require_once($file_name);
    $ct_name = ucfirst($url[0]);
    $controller = new $ct_name;

    if(empty($url[1])){
      $controller->get();
      return false;
}

    $action_name  = isset($url[1]) ? $url[1]:NULL;

    if($action_name && method_exists($controller, $action_name)){
      if(empty($url[2])){
        $controller->{$url[1]}();
      }
```

```
        else{
          $controller->{$url[1]}($url[2]);
        }
      }
    else{
      //should be logged
      //replace the message
      //redirect the user to a custom 404 page
      echo "Action does not exist";


    }


  }
}
```

In the preceding code snippet, we begin by retrieving the data in the url parameter. We begin by using the explode function to build a list of the incoming data. Before we go further, let us look at the following examples of our URLs to understand the URL structure:

URL	Controller	Action	Params
`http://localhost/student-portal/students/add`	Students	add	-
`http://localhost/student-portal/students/get`	Students	get	-
`http://localhost/student-portal/students/delete/1`	Students	delete	1

From this table, it is clear that the data that will be carried in through the url parameter will have the controller, action, and optional parameter. Our bootstrap class will handle all these cases and the cases where enough data is not present. It is now time to implement this functionality in our index.php page, which is the entry point to our application. Enter the following code in our index.php file:

```php
<?php
require_once("config.php");

function __autoload($class) {
        require LIBRARY . $class .".php";
}

$app = new Bootstrap();

?>
```

In the `index.php` file, we begin by importing the configurations from the `config.php` file. Then we are using the `_autoload` magic function to import all the required classes in the `lib` directory. Once the required library files are loaded (including the `Bootstrap.php` file), we instantiate a bootstrap object that will take the request forward. Now that we have our database configurations loaded into the application, we can create our database library file that will provide the required database operations. In our case, let us keep our database library file simple and extend the PDO class.

Enter the following code in our `lib/Database.php` file:

```php
<?php
class Database extends PDO{
  public function __construct($DB_VENDOR, $DB_HOST, $DB_NAME,
      $DB_USR, $DB_PWD){
  parent::__construct($DB_VENDOR.':host='.$DB_HOST.';
    dbname='.$DB_NAME, $DB_USR, $DB_PWD);
  }
}
```

The next thing to set up would be our base model, base view, and base controller that will carry the base functionality that will be used across models, views, and controllers. The base model class that we will build will be very simple and would create a database object and make it available for the controllers to use it. Let us begin with our base model that would use our database library, present in the `lib/Base_Model.php` file:

```php
<?php
abstract class Base_Model{
  public function __construct(){
    $this->db = new Database(DB_VENDOR, DB_HOST, DB_NAME, DB_USR,
        DB_PWD);
  }
}
```

The `Base_Model` class will be an abstract class as there will not be a need for us to instantiate this class and we will extend this class whenever we would need the functionality in it. This class will serve as the parent class for all the models. In this class, we are instantiating the `Database` class. Now let us build our base view class that will carry the functionality that will help us in controller-view interactions and other view-related functionalities. Enter the following code in our `lib/Base_View.php` file:

```php
<?php
class Base_View{
```

```php
    public function __construct(){

    }
    public function render($name){
        require_once("views/layout/header.php");
        require_once("views/$name.php");
        require_once("views/layout/footer.php");
    }
}
```

In our base view library file, we will create the `render` method that would take the name of the view as an argument and import a view file. We are also importing the header and the footer views that are part of the `views/layout` folder. We have not created them yet, but these will just be the placeholders while we continue to set up our MVC application. Now that we have the base view and base model library files, let us build our base controller library file. Enter the following code in our `lib/Base_Controller.php` file:

```php
<?php
abstract class Base_Controller{

    public function __construct(){
        $this->view = new Base_View();
    }

    public function loadModel($name) {

        $path = 'models/'.$name.'_model.php';

        if (file_exists($path)) {
            require_once("models/$name_model.php");

            $modelName = ucfirst($name)."_Model";
            $this->model = new $modelName();
        }
    }
}
```

The base controller library file will be quite simple and we will be instantiating an object of the `Base_View` class. The view object will be available to all the sub classes that extend the `Base_Controller` class, and will thereby be able to use the `render` function to call specific views. We also have the `loadModel` method that takes the name of the controller and performs a little processing to import the model file. Once the model is loaded, we can use the model object to query the database.

Now that we have set up the base libraries for our MVC application, let us build our first controller. The first controller that we will work with is the `Students` controller. The `Students` controller will house all the application logic for the students. Enter the following code in our `controllers/students.php` file:

```php
<?php
class Students extends Base_Controller{
  public function __construct(){
    parent::__construct();
  }
  public function add(){

  }
  public function get($id=null){

  }
}
```

We begin with a skeleton of the application logic that will be housed in the `Students` controller. We will use the `add` action to add a student to the database and use the `get` action to retrieve one or all of the students in the database.

Adding a student

In this section, we will build our first view that will allow us to add a student to our `course_registry` database. While working with MVC, every action in a controller should have a separate view. As there can be one or more actions in a controller, we will create a `students` subdirectory in the `views` directory. Once we start working on the `courses` controller, we will create another subdirectory in the `views` directory for storing the views for the `courses` controller and add the folloing code in the `views/students/add.php` file:

```php
<div id="addStudent">
<?php
  if(isset($this->id)){
    echo "New user has been successfully added";
  }
?>

<form class="Frm" action="add" method="post">
  <ul>
    <li>
      <label>First Name</label>
      <input name="first_name" placeholder="Enter First Name">
    </li>
```

```
  <li>
    <label>Last Name</label>
    <input name="last_name" placeholder="Enter Last Name">
  </li>
  <li>
    <label>Address</label>
    <textarea name="address" placeholder="Enter Address">
      </textarea>
  </li>
  <li>
    <label>City</label>
      <input name="city" placeholder="Enter City">
  </li>
  <li>
    <label>State</label>
    <input name="state" placeholder="Enter State">
  </li>
  <li>
    <label>Zipcode</label>
    <input name="zip_code" placeholder="Enter Zip Code">
  </li>
  <li>

    <label>User Name</label>
    <input name="username" placeholder="Enter User Name">
  </li>
  <li>
  <label>Password</label>
  <input name="password" type="password" >
  </li>
  <li>
    <input type="submit" name="submit" value="Add Student">
  </li>
  </form>
</div>
```

Now that we have a HTML form to add a student, let us look at the process of handling form submission once the user clicks on the Add Student button. One thing to note from this snippet is that the form will post back to the add action upon submission. Now let us look at how the action renders this form and how the action will handle the post back. Enter the following code in our controllers/students.php file:

```
public function add(){

    if(isset($_POST['submit'])){
```

```
        unset($_POST['submit']);
        $this->view->id = $this->model->addStudent($_POST);
    }


    $this->view->render('students/add');
}
```

In the previous code snippet, we are adding the add action to the Students controller. We are doing three things in the add action; they are as follows:

- We begin by checking whether the form has been submitted
- If the form is submitted, we call the addStudent method to add the student to our database
- Finally, we load the view using the render method that we have created in the Base_View library

Now let us load the form using a browser, the URL to load this form will be http://localhost/student-portal/students/add.

The output is as follows:

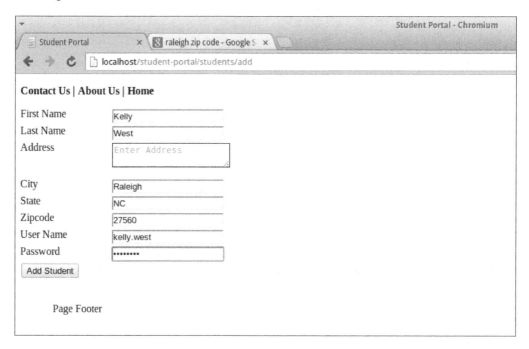

Now once we click the Add Student button, the data will be posted to the add action again. Since $_POST['submit'] will be set to Add Student, the execution will go into the conditional block. Once the post data has been processed, we send it over to the addStudent method in the Students model. Now let us look at how we add the data to the database once the data reaches the model, present in the models/students_model.php file:

```php
<?php
  class Students_Model extends Base_Model{
    public function __construct(){
      parent::__construct();
    }

    public function addStudent($student){
      ksort($student);
      $columns = implode(',', array_keys($student));
      $values = ':' . implode(', :', array_keys($student));

      $stmt = $this->db->prepare("INSERT INTO students
        ($columns) VALUES($values);");
      foreach($student as $key=>$value){
        $stmt->bindValue(":$key", $value);
      }

      $stmt->execute();

      return $this->db->lastInsertId();
    }
  }
```

In the Students model, we begin by extending the Base_Model class. In the addStudent method, we begin by sorting the post data according to the key. We will be using prepared statements to interact with the database. After the key sort, we go through the process of building the insert query. We use the bindValue method to bind the values to the statement. Once the statement is prepared and the values have been bound, we use the execute method to run the query against the database. After a successful execution, we retrieve the ID of the student that has just been added using the lastInsertId method and return it back to controller. This ID is passed across to the view that renders a success message when a student has successfully been added to the database.

The output is as follows:

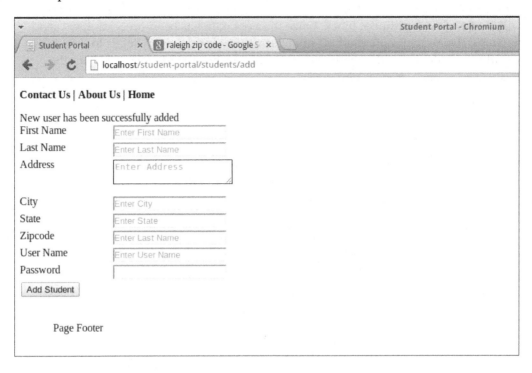

When a user has been successfully added to the database, the **New user has been successfully added** message is displayed on the page. Now that we have added a student to the existing course_registry database, let us retrieve the student ID, the first name, and the last name of all of the students.

Listing all students

Let us continue our work on the Students controller and build an action that would retrieve information about all the students in our students table, present in the controllers/students.php file:

```
public function get($id=null){
  $this->view->student_data = $this->model->getStudents();
  $this->view->render('students/get');
}
```

In this snippet, we are creating the `get` action that retrieves student data. This action can be used to get information about a single student or information about all students.

 We are only handling the case about fetching information about all students; once the portal handles other profile information of the student, we can build a view for the student profile.

We are using the `getStudents` method provided by our `Students_model` to fetch the data and pass it on to the `get.php` view in the `students` subdirectory. Now let us take a quick look at the `getStudents` method, present in the `models/students_model.php` file:

```php
public function getStudents(){
    return $this->db->query("SELECT student_id, first_name,
        last_name FROM students;")->fetchAll(PDO::FETCH_ASSOC);
}
```

In this snippet, we are querying the database to retrieve the student ID, first name, and last name of all the students. We are performing a PDO `fetchAll` to retrieve an array of all the rows. Now this data will be passed back to our `get` action that forwards it over to the `get.php` view. Now let us take a quick look to understand how `get.php` renders the student data, present in the `views/students/get.php` file:

```html
<div id="getStudent">
  <table>
    <tr>
      <th>Student Id</th>
      <th>First Name</th>
      <th>Last Name</th>
    </tr>
    <?php foreach($this->student_data as $student): ?>
      <tr>
        <td><?= $student['student_id']?></td>
        <td><?= $student['first_name']?></td>
        <td><?= $student['last_name']?></td>
      </tr>
    <?php endforeach; ?>
  </table>
</div>
```

In the preceding code snippet, we are using the data stored in `$this->student_data` and are iterating over the array to print the student ID, first name, and last name. Now let us load this page onto the browser. The URL to load this page will be `http://localhost/student-portal/students/get`. The output is as follows:

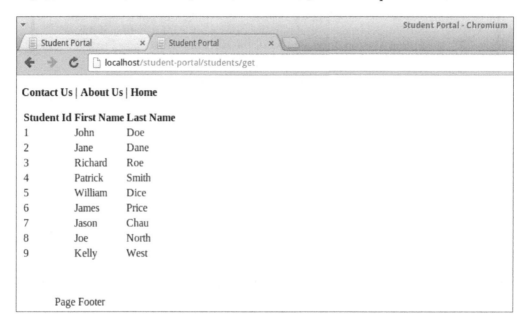

Upon the successful load of this page, we will be able to view the student data in a list format. Now that we have created actions to successfully add and view students. Let us implement the functionality of adding a course and listing all the courses.

Adding a course

In this section, we will add the new `Courses` controller to our controllers' directory. Our `Courses` controller will extend the `Base_Controller` class and, upon instantiation, we will load the `courses` model (we are yet to create the model). The code snippet for the `Courses` controller will be similar to our `Students` controller; this is shown in the following code snippet; in the `controllers/courses.php` file:

```php
<?php
class Courses extends Base_Controller{
  public function __construct(){
    parent::__construct();
    $this->loadModel("courses");
  }
```

```php
    public function add(){

      if(isset($_POST['submit'])){
        unset($_POST['submit']);
        $this->view->id = $this->model->addCourse($_POST);
      }

      $this->view->render('courses/add');
    }
  }
```

We will be using the add action to create a new course and add it to our courses table. In our add action, we are passing in the data in the $_POST superglobal over to the addCourse method provided by our courses model. Now let us look at the addCourse method in our courses model, present in the models/courses_model.php file:

```php
<?php

class Courses_Model extends Base_Model{
  public function __construct(){
    parent::__construct();
  }

  public function addCourse($course){
    ksort($course);
    $columns = implode(',', array_keys($course));
    $values = ':' . implode(', :', array_keys($course));

    $stmt = $this->db->prepare("INSERT INTO courses($columns)
        VALUES($values);");
    foreach($course as $key=>$value){
      $stmt->bindValue(":$key", $value);
    }
    $stmt->execute();

    return $this->db->lastInsertId();
  }
}
```

In this snippet, we have the addCourse method that expects the course data as an argument. Similar to the process of adding a student, we will sort the course data by key and generate the column data and the value data. Later we prepare the insert SQL statement to be run on our course_registry database. Upon a successful insert operation, the last inserted ID is returned back to the controller. The controller will pass this ID to the view, and the view will print the success message that the new course has been successfully added.

Let us now look at our view to add a new course, in the `views/courses/add.php` file:

```php
<div>
<?php
  if(isset($this->id)){
    echo "New course has been successfully added";
  }
?>

<form class="Frm" action="add" method="post">
  <ul>
    <li>
      <label>Course Name</label>
      <input name="name" placeholder="Enter Course Name">
    </li>
    <li>
      <label>Description</label>
      <textarea name="description" placeholder=
        "Enter Description"></textarea>
    </li>
    <li>
      <input type="submit" name="submit" value="Add Course">
    </li>
  </form>
</div>
```

In this snippet, we have an HTML form with two fields for course name and course description. Upon clicking the Add Course button, the data will be submitted to the add action. The add action then forwards the data to the addCourse method in the courses model that adds this new course to the database. The output is as follows:

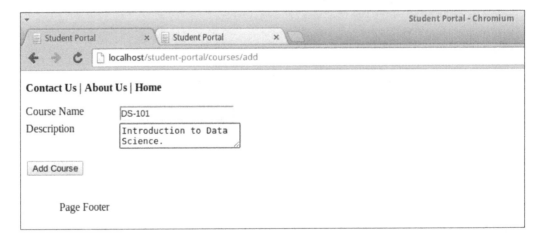

In the preceding screenshot, we are adding the new course, **DS-101**, to our database. In the next section, we will look at how to build a list of all the courses available in the database.

Listing all courses

In this section, we will focus on listing all the courses in the database on the page. We will begin by adding the get action to our Courses controller that will use the getCourses method provided by the courses model. Once the data is retrieved from the getCourses method, the data is forwarded to the get.php view from our get action in the controllers/courses.php file:

```php
public function get($id=null){
  $this->view->course_data = $this->model->getCourses();
  $this->view->render('courses/get');
}
```

The code of the models/courses_model.php file is as follows:

```php
public function getCourses(){
  return $this->db->query("SELECT course_id, name,
    description FROM courses;")->fetchAll(PDO::FETCH_ASSOC);
}
```

The code of the views/courses/get.php file is as follows:

```php
<div id="getCourses">
  <table>
    <tr>
      <th>Course Id</th>
      <th>Course Name</th>
      <th>Description</th>
    </tr>
    <?php foreach($this->course_data as $course): ?>
    <tr>
      <td><?= $course['course_id']?></td>
      <td><?= $course['name']?></td>
      <td><?= $course['description']?></td>
    </tr>
    <?php endforeach; ?>
  </table>
</div>
```

Now let us load this page onto the browser to verify if the **DS-101** course is displayed in this list. The output of the `views/courses/get.php` file is as follows:

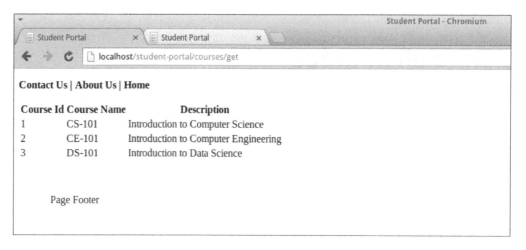

Registering a student to a course

In this section, we will register a student for a course. We will allow the users to register a student to a course by accepting the student ID and course ID. We will add the new `StudentsCourses` controller to our `controllers` directory and it will extend the `Base_Controller` class. Upon instantiation, we will load the `StudentCourses` model (similar to other controllers in the application) in the `controllers/studentsCourses.php` file:

```php
<?php
class StudentsCourses extends Base_Controller{
  public function __construct(){
    parent::__construct();
    $this->loadModel("studentsCourses");
  }

  public function register(){

    if(isset($_POST['submit'])){
      unset($_POST['submit']);
      $student_id = $_POST['student_id'];
      $course_id = $_POST['course_id'];
      $this->view->id = $this->model->registerStudentCourse
        ($student_id, $course_id);
    }
```

```php
    $this->view->render('studentsCourses/register');
  }
}
```

We will be using the `register` action to register a student for a course and add the registration information to our `student_courses` table. In our `register` action, we are extracting the student ID and course ID from the `$_POST` superglobal. We pass these values to the `registerStudentCourse` method provided by our `StudentCourses` model. Now let us look at the `registerStudentCourse` method in our `StudentCourses` model in the `models/studentsCourses_model.php` file:

```php
<?php

class StudentsCourses_Model extends Base_Model{
  public function __construct(){
    parent::__construct();
  }

    public function registerStudentCourse
      ($student_id, $course_id){

    $stmt = $this->db->prepare("INSERT INTO students_course
      (student_id, course_id) VALUES(:student_id, :course_id)");
    $stmt->bindValue(":student_id",$student_id);
    $stmt->bindValue(":course_id",$course_id);
    $stmt->execute();
  }
}
```

In the preceding code snippet, we have the `registerStudentCourse` method that expects the student ID and course ID as arguments. Later, we prepare the insert SQL statement that will register a student for a course. Let us now look at our view to register a student to a new course, in the `views/studentsCourses/register.php` file:

```php
<div>
<?php
  if(isset($this->id)){
    echo "Student has been successfully registered for the
      course";
  }
?>

<form class="Frm" action="register" method="post">
  <ul>
    <li>
      <label>Course Id</label>
```

```
      <input name="course_id" placeholder="Enter Course Id">
    </li>
    <li>
      <label>Student Id</label>
      <input name="student_id" placeholder="Enter Student Id"/>
    </li>
    <li>
      <input type="submit" name="submit" value="Register Course">
    </li>
  </ul>
</form>
</div>
```

In this snippet, we provide two textboxes for the users to enter the student ID and the course ID. On clicking the `Register Course` button, the student will be registered to the specific course. Now let us load this page onto the browser to view the output. The URL to load this page will be `http://localhost/student-portal/studentsCourses/register`. The output is as follows:

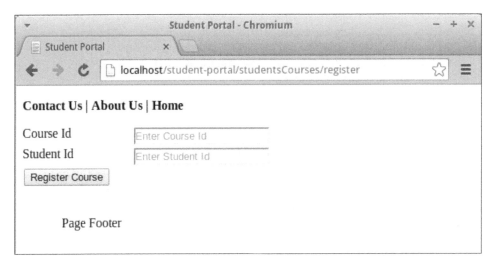

Now that we have this page to register a student for a course, let us look at the screen to view all the registrations.

Viewing all registrations

In this section, we will build the screen that would retrieve all the current registrations in our `course_registry` database. We will begin by adding the `get` action to our `StudentsCourses` controller that will use the `getStudentsCourses` method provided by the `StudentCourses` model. Once the data is retrieved from the `getStudentsCourses` method, the data is forwarded to the `get.php` view from our `get` action. Let us add these methods to the existing scripts. The code in the `controllers/studentsCourses.php` file is as follows:

```
public function get(){
  $this->view->studentsCourses_data =
    $this->model->getStudentsCourses();
  $this->view->render('studentsCourses/get');
}
```

The code in the `models/studentsCourses_model.php` file is as follows:

```
public function getStudentsCourses(){
  $stmt = $this->db->prepare("SELECT s.first_name, s.last_name,
    s.student_id, c.course_id, c.name as course_name
    FROM students_courses sc INNER JOIN students s ON
    sc.student_id=s.student_id INNER JOIN courses c ON
    sc.course_id=c.course_id");


    $stmt->execute();

    $studentsCourses = [];
    while($row = $stmt->fetch(PDO::FETCH_ASSOC)){
      $studentsCourses[] = $row;
    }

    return $studentsCourses;
    }
```

The code in the `views/studentsCourses/get.php` file is as follows:

```
<div id="getStudentCourses">
  <table>
    <tr>
      <th>First Name</th>
      <th>Last Name</th>
```

```
      <th>Course Name</th>
    </tr>
    <?php foreach($this->studentsCourses_data as $
      studentCourseData): ?>
      <tr>
        <td><?= $studentCourseData['first_name']?></td>
        <td><?= $studentCourseData['last_name']?></td>
        <td><?= $studentCourseData['course_name']?></td>
      </tr>
    <?php endforeach; ?>
  </table>
</div>
```

Now that we have added the required scripts to fetch the existing registrations and to render them onto the browser, let us load this page into the browser. The URL to load this page onto the browser is `http://localhost/student-portal/studentsCourses/get`. The output is as follows:

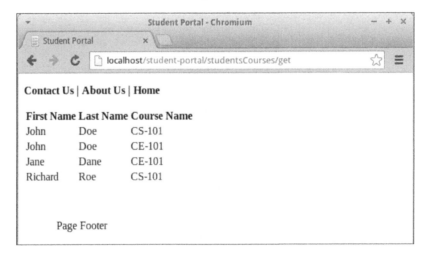

In the preceding screenshot, we are rendering the list of existing registrations that are available in our `course_registry` database. We have covered many tasks for our student application; a few similar tasks that we will tackle in *Chapter 6, Authentication and Access Control*, are as follows:

- Deregistering a student from a course
- Deleting a student
- Deleting a course

We have successfully laid the foundational work towards building our student application. Now let us go over a few files that I have mentioned briefly but did not go through in any length. These files are as follows:

- **header.php**: The header section of all the pages will be coming from this file. This file can be split further to have a partial view file that will be specifically used for holding the navigation system and to dynamically accept a page-specific title. This file is located in the `views/layouts/` subdirectory.

- **footer.php**: The footer section of all the pages will be coming from this file. This file is located in the `views/layouts/` subdirectory.

- **styles.css**: This file will be used as the main CSS file for our student portal application. A good feature to implement is partial- or controller-specific CSS files. The file is referenced in the `header.php` file.

Both the `header.php` and `footer.php` files are used for view generation, which is performed by the `render` method in the `Base_View` library class. Now let us look at the folder structure and all the files that will be part of the code bundle for this chapter, as shown in the following screenshot:

```
├── assets
│   └── css
│       └── styles.css
├── config.php
├── controllers
│   ├── courses.php
│   └── students.php
├── index.php
├── lib
│   ├── Base_Controller.php
│   ├── Base_Model.php
│   ├── Base_View.php
│   ├── Bootstrap.php
│   └── Database.php
├── models
│   ├── courses_model.php
│   └── students_model.php
└── views
    ├── courses
    │   ├── add.php
    │   └── get.php
    ├── layout
    │   ├── footer.php
    │   └── header.php
    └── students
        ├── add.php
        └── get.php
```

Summary

In this chapter, we began by building our student portal application that can be used to add students, view a list of students, add courses, view a list of courses that are available, register a student to a course, and to view all the registrations in the database. During this chapter, we built our own MVC framework. There are a lot of MVC frameworks that are already available; for any application development purpose, it is advised to use an existing MVC framework as it would be thoroughly tested and will have been extensively used by others. The MVC framework that we during this chapter should be used as a reference to understand the nuts and bolts of existing MVC frameworks. In the next chapter, we will go over common file operations and how PHP allows us to interact with files.

5
Working with Files and Directories

In the last chapter, we discussed the basics of building our student portal application. In this chapter, we will focus on file interactions and operations. PHP allows us to work with files that are available both locally and on a remote server. Files are commonly used to store logs and configurations of an application. They are also used to carry data from one application to another. In this chapter, we will begin by working with data imports from files and data exports to files. Later, we will look at two different types of logging mechanisms that will take us further with our interaction with files.

Data imports

In real-world applications, data may have to be consumed from multiple sources, and a lot of applications are still built to use flat files for data storage. In this section, we will work with a file containing data about students, and import that data into our `course_registry` database. There are multiple formats that are commonly used to store data in a flat file. These formats use delimiters such as a comma, tab, or space, to separate one data item from another. The most popular formats are the **CSV (comma separated values)** and **TSV (tab separated values)** formats. We will work with a comma-separated list of student data that is stored in a flat file. Let's take a quick look at this data.

The following code snippet is contained in the `students.csv` file:

```
George,Johnson,3225 Woodland Park Dr,Houston,TX,77087,george.johnson,
6579e96f76baa00787a28653876c6127
Charles,Davis,3225 Woodland Park Dr,Houston,TX,77087,charles.davis,
6579e96f76baa00787a28653876c6127
```

```
Edward,Moore,3225 Woodland Park Dr,Houston,TX,77087,edward.moore,
6579e96f76baa00787a28653876c6127
Brian,Anderson,3225 Woodland Park Dr,Houston,TX,77087,brian.anderson,
6579e96f76baa00787a28653876c6127
```

This file contains the data about four new students that we would like to add to our existing `students` table. This data includes the first names, last names, addresses, cities, states, zip codes, user names, and the SHA1 hashes of the students' passwords. To import this file, we need to have at least two things: a form to upload this file and an action that would take this file, extract the data, and call the appropriate function in the model to add this data to our `course_registry` database.

Let's begin by building the form that will allow a user to upload this file. Since the file import functionality will not be used often, let's make this form toggleable so that it will appear upon clicking a link. We will add the `ImportStudents` link, and then add the toggle functionality to this link, so that the form will appear upon clicking this link. We will add the link and form to the `get.php` view.

The following code snippet is contained in the `views/students/get.php` file:

```php
<div id="getStudent">
  <div id="importStudents">
    <p>
      <a id="importStudentsLink" href="#">Import Students</a>
    </p>
    <div style="clear:both"></div>
    <div id="importStudentsFrm" style="display:none;">
      <form action="/student-portal/students/import" method="post"
        enctype="multipart/form-data">
        <label for="file"></label>
        <input type="file" name="file" />
        <input type="submit" name="submit" value=
          "Import Students" />
      </form>
    </div>
  </div>
  <div id="message">
    <?php if(isset($this->message)): ?>
    <?= $this->message ?>
    <?php endif; ?>
  </div>
  <table>
    <tr>
      <th>Student Id</th>
      <th>First Name</th>
```

```
        <th>Last Name</th>
      </tr>
      <?php foreach($this->student_data as $student): ?>
      <tr>
        <td><?= $student['student_id']?></td>
        <td><?= $student['first_name']?></td>
        <td><?= $student['last_name']?></td>
      </tr>
      <?php endforeach; ?>
    </table>
  </div>
```

We have made a few changes to the existing get.php view, the first being the addition of the Import Students link. We are not giving a value to the href attribute because this link will only be used to show the upload form that will allow the user to upload the student data. We use a very simple upload form that allows the user to pick a file and click on the submit button to upload the file to the server. We use the HTTP POST method to upload the file, and we mention that the encoding type should be multipart/form-data that allows the data being submitted (including the files) to be encoded and sent to the server in the POST body. We are going to submit this data to our new import action. Let's load this view into the browser and look at the form now. The output is as follows:

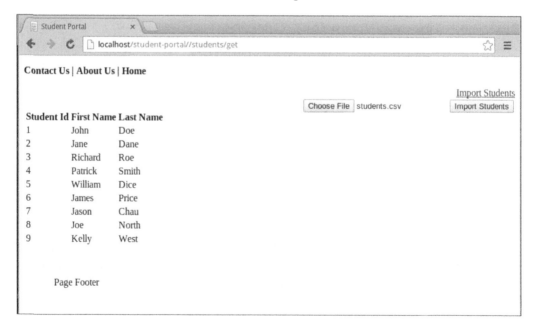

Here we load the page into the browser and click on the Import Students link to load the upload form. Now, we use the Choose File button to pick the students.csv file that contains the student data, and upon form submission, this data is sent to the server.

The students.csv file is part of the code files.

Let's look at how the file handling is performed once the file reaches the server. The following code needs to be entered in the controllers/students.php file:

```php
public function import(){
  if(isset($_POST['submit'])){
    if($_FILES['file']['error']==0){
      if (($handle = fopen($_FILES['file']['tmp_name'], 'r'))
         !== FALSE) {
        while (($data = fgetcsv($handle, 1000, ',')) !== FALSE) {
          $student['first_name'] = $data[0];
          $student['last_name'] = $data[1];
          $student['address'] = $data[2];
          $student['city'] = $data[3];
          $student['state'] = $data[4];
          $student['zip_code'] = $data[5];
          $student['username'] = $data[6];
          $student['password'] = $data[7];

          $this->model->addStudent($student);
        }
      }

      header('Location:'.BASE_URL.
        '/students/get?message=importSuccess');
    }
  }
}
```

In this snippet, we add the import action to the students controller. The import action will be responsible for parsing the file and extracting the data. In the import action, we begin by checking if the form was successfully submitted. We then use the $_FILES superglobal provided by PHP to retrieve the information of the file that was uploaded. When a file is uploaded via a form, this file is stored in the temporary directory, and we will normally use the move_uploaded_file function to relocate the file to a directory that can store the file persistently.

In our case, we are only concerned with extracting the information from the file, and we will not store the file locally. We will create a file resource to the file in the temporary directory and open the file in read mode. As we are uploading a CSV file, we can use the fgetcsv function provided by PHP to extract the information from the file. Using the fgetcsv function, we read one line at a time and pass the data to our addStudent function provided by our students model.

> It is recommended to verify the file type of the uploaded file using $_FILES['file']['type'] before using the fgetcsv function. We are assuming that the student information is provided in CSV format.

Upon completion of inserting data into the students table, we will use the header function provided by PHP to redirect the user to the get action. By redirecting the user to the get action, we allow the user to make sure that the student data has been successfully added. Now that we understand how the data in the students.csv file is handled, let's upload the file and verify if the data has been loaded into the database. The output will be as follows:

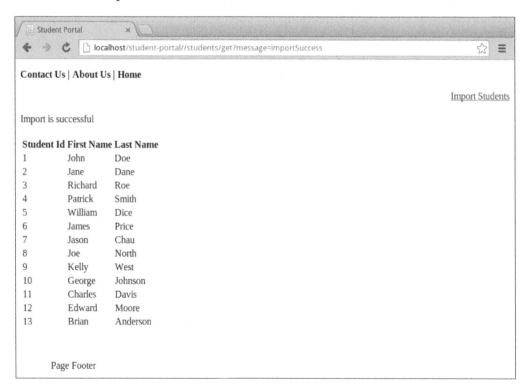

Upon a successful import operation, we will receive a success message that says **Import is successful**. Now that we can see the list of students, we can verify if any new student has been added to the database.

Data exports

Now that we have successfully imported data into our database, let's look at the process for exporting the data. In this section, we will look at two tasks: exporting the data to a file in the local filesystem and allowing a user to download that exported file. Let's begin by making a small change to the get.php view to add a link to export the data, using the following code. We will add the following line of code to the paragraph tag that contains the Import Students link:

```
<a id="exportStudentsLink" href="export">Export Students</a>
```

Here, we set the href attribute to the export action that we will be adding. As the name suggests, we will use the export action to export the student data into a CSV file, and allow the users to download this data. Before we go over the export action, we need to make three updates to the existing code. The first change will be to add a constant that will hold the root-working directory to our config.php file that houses our configurations:

```
define('ROOT_DIR', dirname(__FILE__));
```

In this snippet, we use the __FILE__ magic constant to retrieve the name of the existing file, and then use the dirname function provided by PHP to get the path to our root directory. The next change that we will make is to modify the getStudents method in our students_model to return all columns in the students table, as shown in the following code:

```
public function getStudents(){
  return $this->db->query("SELECT * FROM students;")
    ->fetchAll(PDO::FETCH_ASSOC);
}
```

We will finally add the files directory to house the files that our application will use in the controllers/students.php file, as shown in the following code snippet:

```
public function export(){
  $data = $this->model->getStudents();
  $handle = fopen(ROOT_DIR.'/assets/files/students.csv', 'w+');
```

```
  foreach ($data as $student) {
    fputcsv($handle, array($student['student_id'],
      $student['first_name'], $student['last_name'],
      $student['address'],$student['city'],$student['state']));
  }
  fclose($handle);

  header('Content-Disposition: attachment;
    filename="students.csv"');
  header('Content-Type:application/csv');

  readfile(ROOT_DIR.'/assets/files/students.csv');
}
```

In this action, we begin by fetching the student data using the `getStudents` method from our `students` model. We use the `ROOT_DIR` constant to open a new file handle in the write mode, and use the `fputcsv` function to add data in the CSV format. Later, to allow the user to download this file, we will pass HTTP headers that will denote to the browser that this file is an attachment, and we will set the filename in that header. The last header that we will pass is to let the browser know about the content type of the data that is coming over from the server. We will use the `readfile` function to retrieve the information from the file and pass it to the browser.

Logging

The last file operation that we will work with is logging. We will begin by looking at how information can be logged to web server logs and build a simple logging library that can be used across the application. Let's begin by using the `error_log` function provided by PHP to log information into the web server logfiles. For this example, let's use the export action that we created in the last section to add a message that will be logged.

The following codec needs to be added to the `controllers/students.php` file:

```
public function export(){
  $data = $this->model->getStudents();
  $handle = fopen(ROOT_DIR.'/assets/files/students.csv', 'w+');
  foreach ($data as $student) {
    fputcsv($handle, array($student['student_id'],
      $student['first_name'], $student['last_name'],
      $student['address'],$student['city'],$student['state']));
  }
  fclose($handle);
```

```
header('Content-Disposition: attachment;
   filename="students.csv"');
header('Content-Type:application/csv');

readfile(ROOT_DIR.'/assets/files/students.csv');
error_log('Students.csv has been successfully exported');
}
```

Now, let's click on the `Export Students` link again to export the student data. To view the log messages, we will have to open up the `error.log` file that is used by the web server. For an Apache web server, the server logs are stored in the `/var/log/apache2/` directory. The output will be as follows:

```
[Sun Mar 30 17:25:11.870341 2014] [:error] [pid 5439] [client
127.0.0.1:55111] Students.csv has been successfully exported, referer:
http://localhost/student-portal/students/get
```

One thing to note is that we do not have a lot of control from the application over what message is logged to the server logs. Logging is often used with rapid prototyping and development. If we want to log any debugging information or a warning, it will be logged as an error when it is not really an error. To gain more control over the logging structure, let's go ahead and build a simple logger class that will allow us to log messages and have a clear differentiation between a debugging information message, a warning, and an error. Before we begin with work on our logger library file, let's add the path to the directory into which the logfiles are saved:

```
define('LOG_PATH',ROOT_DIR.'/logs/');
```

We use the `ROOT_DIR` constant that we had set up in the previous section to build the path to the directory that will house the logs. Now, let's build our logger library, which will be in the path `lib/Logger.php`, using the following code snippet:

```php
<?php
class Logger{
  public function __construct(){
    $this->path = LOG_PATH;
  }

  private function log($type, $message){
    $handle = fopen($this->path."app.log","a+");
    fwrite($handle, $type." : ".$message.PHP_EOL);
    fclose($handle);
```

```
    }

    public function info($message){
        $this->log("info",$message);
    }

    public function warn($message){
        $this->log("warn",$message);
    }

    public function error($message){
        $this->log("error",$message);
    }
}
```

In the `Logger` library class, we begin with adding a constructor and setting the path to a class variable. We then move on to our `log` private method that will be used by the rest of the public logging methods in our class. This `log` method will take two arguments, the first argument is the type of the log item and the second argument is the message of the log item. In this method, we begin by opening a file handle that will open the `app.log` file in the `append` mode. We use this file handle to write the type and message of the log item. Once the log item is written to the file, we will close the file handle. This log method can now be used by other wrapper methods, and they will pass in the type and message for the log item. Now that we have our `Logger` library, let's use this logger to log a few messages. To access our `Logger`, we will create an object to the logger in our `Base_Controller` library class:

```
public function __construct(){
    $this->view = new Base_View();
    $this->logger = new Logger();
}
```

In this snippet, we create an object for the `Logger` library class and assign that to a class variable that will be available for all the classes that will extend the `Base_Controller` class. Let's use the `$this->logger` class variable in the `export` action in our `students` controller. We will replace the existing call to `error_log` function with a call to info methods provided by our `Logger` library, using the following code snippet:

```
public function export(){
    $data = $this->model->getStudents();
    $handle = fopen(ROOT_DIR.'/assets/files/students.csv', 'w+');
    foreach ($data as $student) {
```

```
        fputcsv($handle, array($student['student_id'],
            $student['first_name'], $student['last_name']
            ,$student['address'],$student['city'],$student['state']));
    }
    fclose($handle);

    header('Content-Disposition: attachment;
        filename="students.csv"');
    header('Content-Type:application/csv');

    readfile(ROOT_DIR.'/assets/files/students.csv');
    $this->logger->info("Students.csv has been successfully
        exported");
}
```

The only change that has been made to the export action is the replacement of the call to the `error_log` function with the info method provided by our `Logger` library. Now, let's export the student data one more time and see if the message is logged to the `app.log` file located in the `logs` directory. The output will be as follows:

```
info : Students.csv has been successfully exported
```

Now that we have an idea of how a logger library works, it is always recommended to use a third-party library such as *log4php* for application-logging purposes.

Summary

In this chapter, we discussed working with file imports and file exports, and then we looked at how logging can be performed in our application. In the next chapter, we will go over authentication and access control lists.

6
Authentication and Access Control

In the previous chapter, we went over basic file operations such as importing data from files, exporting information to files, and logging data to files. In this chapter, we will go over the basics of how authentication and access control can be implemented into our application. Our student portal application can now perform three major tasks: the first is to add a student, the next is to add a course, and the third is to register a student to a course. Till now, we have a universal user that can do any of these operations. In this chapter, we will modify this behavior to set up session handling, access controls, and user roles for these users. We will use sessions to persist user data and provide a personalized experience when they login. The topics that we will discuss in this chapter are:

- Authentication
- Access controls
- User roles

Authentication

It is very common to track and store user information in cookies; however, since cookies are stored on the client side, we will use sessions for storing user information and making it available across the web application after authenticating the users. We will still use authentication for determining whether the submitted data is valid. Upon authentication, we will load the required user information into session variables and use that information wherever required. For building authentication for our student portal, let us begin by creating our library files to support the authentication.

Create the `lib/Session.php` file with the following code:

```php
<?php

class Session
{

  public static function init()
  {
    session_start();
  }
  public static function destroy()
  {
    session_destroy();
  }

}
```

In this snippet, we begin creating the Session library that contains two methods, init and destroy. The init and destroy functions use the session_start and session_destroy functions provided by PHP. As the name suggests, a session is started when the session_start function is executed. A unique session identifier is generated by the web server that is used to identify this session. Whenever a request is made to get or set a session variable pertaining to that particular session, the web server would need the session ID to identify this session. The second method in our Session library is the destroy method that would invoke the session_destroy function that ends the current session. Now that we know how to create and destroy a session, let us build utility methods that would set and get session variables:

```php
public static function set($key, $value)
{
  $_SESSION[$key] = $value;
}

public static function get($key)
{
  if(isset($_SESSION[$key])){
    return $_SESSION[$key];
  }
  else{
    return false;
  }
}
```

In the aforementioned snippet, we begin with the set method that will set a session variable into the $_SESSION superglobal. The session variables are stored as serialized objects in a file, this file is stored in the /tmp directory by default. To explicitly specify a directory that should store the sessions, we will have to make the following configuration change in the /etc/php5/apache2/php.ini file:

```
session.save_path = "/var/apache2/sessions"
```

The next method that we will work with is the get method that will retrieve the values of session variables from the $_SESSION superglobal. The $_SESSION superglobal carries the session variables and makes the variables available across the web application. Now that we have built our Session library, let us build our login controller that will use our Session library to handle the login functionality. The login controller will contain a landing page to allow the users to submit their username and password. It will also have utility functions to process logins and logouts. In the following code snippet, we begin by creating our Login controller that will extend the Base_Controller class:

```php
<?php
class Login extends Base_Controller {

    function __construct() {
        parent::__construct();
        Session::init();
        $this->loadModel('login');
    }

    function index()
    {
        $username = Session::get('username');
        $this->view->username = $username?$username:'';
        $this->view->message = isset($_GET['message'])?
            $_GET['message']:'';
        $this->view->render('login/index');
    }

    function runLogout()
    {
        Session::destroy();
```

```
        header('Location: ' . BASE_URL .
            'login/index?message='.urlencode('logout success'));
    }

    function runLogin()
    {
      $username = $_POST['username'];
      $password = $_POST['password'];
      $this->model->login($username, $password);
    }
  }
}
```

In the constructor of the `login.php` file, we will use the `init` method from our `Session` library to start the session or continue an existing session. We are also using the `loadModel` method to load the `login` model. In the `index` action, we begin by checking to see if a `username` is part of the session variables. Now let us look at the `index` view that we will render for this action:

```html
<h1>Login</h1>
<?php
  echo 'This is the username of the logged in user: '.
    $this->username;
  echo '<br />';
  echo 'This is the message: '.$this->message;
  echo '<br />';
?>
<form class="Frm" action="runLogin" method="post">
  <ul>
  <li>
    <label>Username</label>
    <input name="username" placeholder="Enter User Name">
  </li>
  <li>
    <label>Password</label>
    <input name="password" type="password" placeholder=
      "Enter Password">
  </li>
  </ul>
    <input type="submit" name="submit" value="Login">
  </li>
</form>
```

The `index.php` file is a very simple login form that will allow the user to enter username and password. Upon form submission, the data is posted to the `runLogin` method in our `Login` controller. In the `runLogin` method, the posted data is retrieved and is passed to the `login` method in `Login_Model`. Let us look at our `Login_Model` method to understand how this data is processed to check if the user exists in the database and if there is a match of the username and password combination. In the following code snippet, we begin by creating the `Login_Model` class that carries the login method. The `models/login_model.php` file is modified as follows:

```php
<?php

class Login_Model extends Base_Model{
  public function __construct(){
    parent::__construct();
  }

  public function login($username, $password){
    $st = $this->db->prepare("SELECT username FROM students WHERE
      username = :username AND password = :password");
    $st->execute(array(
      ':username' => $username,
      ':password' => SHA1($password)
      ));

    $data = $st->fetch(PDO::FETCH_ASSOC);
    $hasData = $st->rowCount();

    if($hasData >0){
      Session::set('loggedin',true);
      Session::set('username',$data['username']);
      header('Location:'. BASE_URL. 'students/get?message=
        '.urlencode('login successful'));
    }
    else{

      header('Location:'. BASE_URL.
        'login/index?message='.urlencode('login failed'));
    }
  }
}
```

The login method accepts the username and the password for the user. We will begin by querying the students table with this username and password. If the username of the user is returned, we will set the username and a flag to denote that the user is logged-in to the session data. After setting the session variables, we will redirect the user to the students/get page upon success and redirect the user to the login page to allow the user to login again. Now let us look at the login page and use the credentials of John Doe to login. This is shown in the following screenshot:

The final code change that we'll make will be to the header to add a logout link that will use our runLogout method, which will invoke the destroy method from our Session library. In the following snippet, we are adding the username of the currently logged-in user and the logout link for the user to logout to the header section. The views/layout/header.php file is modified with the following code:

```
<header>
  <p class="iblk">Contact Us | About Us | Home</p>
  <?php if(Session::get("loggedin")): ?>
    <p class="iblk log"><?= Session::get("username")." | "?>
      <a href=<?= BASE_URL."login/runLogout"?>>Logout</a></p>
  <?php endif;?>
</header>
```

Let us look at the following screenshot once the user is logged in:

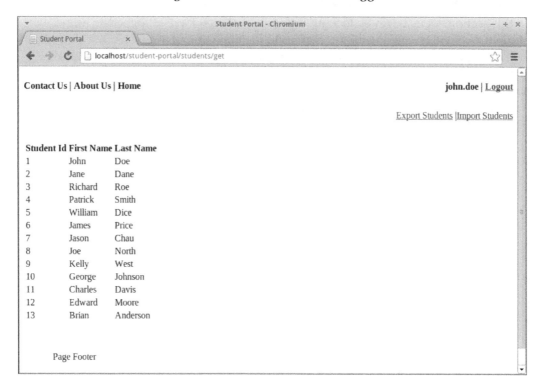

Now that we have successfully logged-in as a user, let us start defining the sections of the application that can be accessed by a user and lock down the access for the rest of the application. The two examples that we will discuss in the next section are:

- A user logged-in as a student should not be able to add a course
- Students should only be able to register themselves but not anybody else

Access controls

In this section, let us begin by locking down the access for a user logged-in as a student. We will be making a few changes to facilitate this change. The first change will be adding new session variables to carry more information about the user. We will make this change to the login method in the Login_Model class. In the following snippet, we have modified the SQL to fetch the username and student ID. We are then adding the student ID to the session variables in the models/login_model.php file, as shown in the following code:

```
public function login($username, $password){
  $st = $this->db->prepare("SELECT student_id, username FROM
    students WHERE username = :username AND password
    = :password");
  $st->execute(array(
    ':username' => $username,
    ':password' => SHA1($password)
    ));

  $data = $st->fetch(PDO::FETCH_ASSOC);
  $hasData = $st->rowCount();

  if($hasData >0){
    Session::set('loggedin',true);
    Session::set('username',$data['username']);
    Session::set('role','student');
    Session::set('student_id', $data['student_id']);
    header('Location:'. BASE_URL. 'students/
      get?message='.urlencode('login successful'));
  }
  else{

    header('Location:'. BASE_URL. 'login
      /index?message='.urlencode('login failed'));
  }
}
```

The final change to the login method is to add a role to the session variables. At this point, we only have a single type of user, a student. Therefore, we can go ahead and add it directly. We will come back to make this more dynamic in the next section. Now that we have added this information to the session variables, let us update the add action in the Courses controller. In the following snippet, we begin by retrieving the role of the user that is currently logged-in. The changes made in the controllers/courses.php file are as follows:

```
public function add(){
  $role = Session::get('role');
```

```
if($role && $role!='student'){
    if(isset($_POST['submit'])){
    unset($_POST['submit']);
    $this->view->id = $this->model->addCourse($_POST);
  }

  $this->view->render('courses/add');
  }
  else{
    header('Location:'.BASE_URL.'students/get?message='
      .urlencode('Students cannot add courses'));
  }
}
```

Our conditional statement verifies that the logged-in user is not a student before rendering the view that allows the user to add a course. If the user is a student, they will be redirected back to the get action for the `Students` controller; this prints the message **Students cannot add courses** on the screen as shown in the following screenshot:

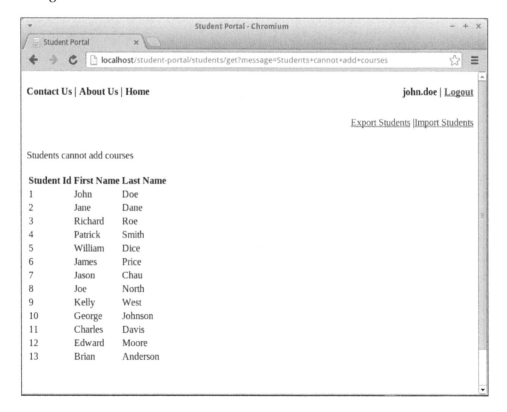

From the previous output, we can verify that the user tried to access the add action of the Courses controller and was redirected to the get action of the Students controller. Now let us continue to our next task of locking down students from registering anybody but themselves for a course. In the current application, as we do not have a lot of access controls, a student can register anyone for a course. By using their student IDs stored in the session variables, we will be negating this issue. We will begin by modifying the register action in the StudentsCourses controller. In the following snippet of the controllers/studentsCourses.php file, we are checking to retrieve the role of the user from the session:

```php
public function register(){

    if(isset($_POST['submit'])){
        unset($_POST['submit']);
        $student_id = $_POST['student_id'];
        $course_id = $_POST['course_id'];
        $this->view->id = $this->model->registerStudentCourse
            ($student_id, $course_id);
    }

    $role = Session::get('role');

    if($role == 'student'){
        $this->view->student_id = Session::get('student_id');
    }

    $this->view->role = $role?$role:'';
    $this->view->render('studentsCourses/register');
}
```

If a role exists in the session variables for this user, the role is returned, if not, false is returned. After we retrieve the role, we are checking to see if the user is a student; if it is, we are retrieving the student ID of the user and passing it on to the view. Now let us look at the changes that we will make to the view in order to restrict a user from registering anyone else other than themselves. In the following snippet of the views/studentsCourses/register.php file, we are modifying the script to render the student ID in a label, thereby not allowing the logged-in user to directly modify the student ID or register another user for a course:

```php
<div>
<?php
    if(isset($this->id)){
        echo "Student has been successfully registered
            for the course";
    }
?>
```

```
<form class="Frm" action="register" method="post">
  <ul>
    <li>
      <label>Course Id</label>
      <input name="course_id" placeholder="Enter Course Id">
    </li>
    <li>
      <label>Student Id</label>
      <?php if($this->role != 'student'):?>
      <input name="student_id" placeholder="Enter Student Id"/>
      <?php else: ?>
      <label><?= $this->student_id ?></label>
      <input name="student_id" type="hidden" value
        =<?= $this->student_id?>/>
      <?php endif;?>
    </li>
    <li>
      <input type="submit" name="submit" value="Register Course">
    </li>
  </ul>
  </form>
</div>
```

Now let's render the following page to verify our changes:

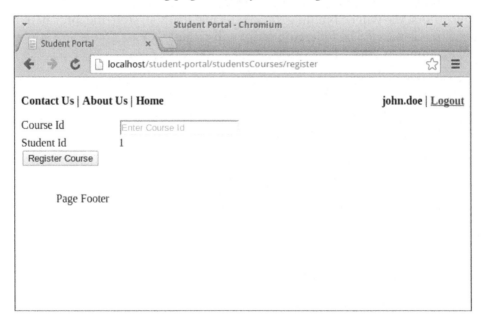

From the output, we can verify that the logged-in users cannot register anybody apart from themselves as the student ID field is no longer a textbox.

 The student ID field has been converted from a textbox to hidden input, so this completely does not prevent the logged-in user from changing the student ID before registering from a course. In *Chapter 9, Security*, we will fix this issue by making this check on the server, rather than on the client.

Now that we have laid down the access rules, let's set up a new user role as an administrator. The two examples that we will discuss in the next section are:

* Adding courses
* Registering students for courses

User roles

In this section, let's begin by creating administrators who will have access across the student portal and will be able to perform operations such as adding courses and registering any student for a course. Let's begin by creating a few administrators. We will be building an `admin` table that will store the information for the administrators. The following script will create the `admin` table and add a couple of administrators. The script is saved as the `assets/sql/admin.sql` file:

```
CREATE TABLE IF NOT EXISTS 'admin' (
  'admin_id' int(11) NOT NULL AUTO_INCREMENT,
  'name' varchar(45) NOT NULL,
  'username' varchar(45) NOT NULL,
  'password' varchar(45) NOT NULL,
  PRIMARY KEY ('admin_id')
) ENGINE=InnoDB  DEFAULT CHARSET=latin1 AUTO_INCREMENT=3 ;


--
-- Dumping data for table 'admin'
--

INSERT INTO 'admin' ('admin_id', 'name', 'username', 'password')
VALUES
(1, 'admin1', 'admin1', '5f4dcc3b5aa765d61d8327deb882cf99'),
(2, 'admin2', 'admin2', '5f4dcc3b5aa765d61d8327deb882cf99');
```

Now that we have our administrators, let's begin by modifying our login view that will allow both students and administrators to login. As we only have two roles currently in the `views/login/index.php` file, we can add a checkbox to allow administrators to set a flag that we will utilize during the login:

```
<h1>Login</h1>
<?php
  if(Session::get("loggedin")){
    echo 'This is the username of the logged in user: '.
      $this->username;
     echo '<br />';
  }

  if($this->message){
    echo 'This is the message: '.$this->message;
    echo '<br />';
  }
?>
<form class="Frm" action="runLogin" method="post">
  <ul>
  <li>
    <label>Username</label>
    <input name="username" placeholder="Enter User Name">
  </li>
  <li>
    <label>Password</label>
    <input name="password" type="password" placeholder=
      "Enter Password">
  </li>
  <li>
    <label>Admin Login</label>
    <input type="checkbox" name="IsAdmin" />
  </li>
  <li>
  <input type="submit" name="submit" value="Login">
  </li>
</form>
```

In the preceding snippet, we are adding another list item to our login form that will allow the users to login with administrator credentials. If the user is not part of the `admin` table, then the user will not be successfully logged in. Now let's update our `Login_Model` class to accommodate these changes using the following code snippet in the `models/login_model.php` file:

```php
<?php

class Login_Model extends Base_Model{
  public function __construct(){
    parent::__construct();
  }

  public function login($username, $password,$type){
    $st = $this->db->prepare($this->buildQuery($type));
    $st->execute(array(
      ':username' => $username,
      ':password' => SHA1($password)
    ));

    $data = $st->fetch(PDO::FETCH_ASSOC);
    $hasData = $st->rowCount();

    if($hasData >0){
      $this->setSessionVariables($data, $type);
      header('Location:'. BASE_URL. 'students/get?message=
        '.urlencode('login successful'));
    }
    else{
      header('Location:'. BASE_URL. 'login/index?message=
        '.urlencode('login failed'));
    }
  }

  private function buildQuery($type){
    $id = $type.'_id';
```

```
    $table = $type;
    return "SELECT $id, username FROM $table WHERE username =
        :username AND password = :password";
}

private function setSessionVariables($data, $type){
    Session::set('loggedin',true);
    Session::set('username',$data['username']);
    Session::set('role',$type);
    Session::set($type.'_id', $data[$type.'_id']);
  }
}
```

In the preceding code snippet, we have refactored the code into multiple methods to handle the process of dynamically building the query and once the login is successful, we will set the user information to the session variables. Now let's verify if we can add a course as an administrator. The output is shown in the following screenshot:

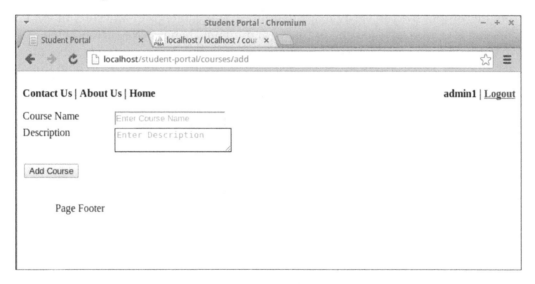

From the output, we can verify that an admin has the access permissions to add a course. Now let's verify if the admin has access to register any student to a course. This can be seen in the following screenshot:

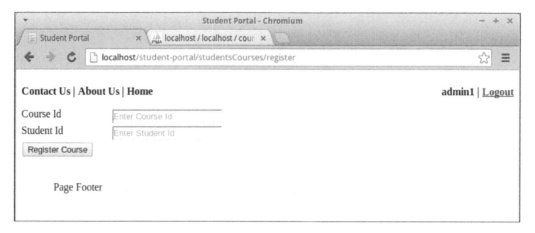

From this output, we can verify that an administrator can register any student for a course and we were able to achieve this with minimal changes. We currently have two types of users; these sorts of operations can get cumbersome as the number of types of users increase. It is advised to use **Access Control Lists** (**ACL**) to hold this information. ACLs are commonly stored in the database and are used to figure out the type of access a user has upon page load or initial login.

Summary

In this chapter, we went over authentication and access controls. We began with authentication and working with sessions to understand how user information can be across various pages on the student portal. Then we introduced access controls where we defined the amount of access for a logged-in user. We continued the development of our student portal by introducing the concept of user roles where the access was different for users with different roles. In the next chapter, we will look at the various types of caching and how caching can help our application.

7
Caching

In the previous chapter, we went over the basics of authentication and access control. We started with an understanding of how a user can be authenticated onto our `student` portal, and then continued to set up access permissions to users. We progressed by creating multiple user roles to utilize the access permissions and restrict access based on the user roles. In this chapter, we will look at different mechanisms to cache the data that we are working with. We will have to consider scaling the application since, at some point, the application will grow bigger and the number of users accessing our `student` portal will increase. Scaling can be done in multiple ways, such as:

- By adding more hardware
- By optimizing our network
- By refactoring our code to perform better and giving it some performance tweaks
- By reducing the number of calls to our database and filesystem

We will cover the last method of scaling in this chapter, while we will go over the third topic in *Chapter 10, Performance Optimization*. We will not go over the rest of the topics since they beyond the scope of this book.

Introduction to caching

Caching can be defined as the process of making popular data highly available by temporarily storing the data in memory. This allows responding to a request faster by retrieving data from the memory rather than going onto the disk. There are three types of caching, as follows:

- Caching in the database
- Caching in the application
- Content caching

Let's begin with database caching.

Caching in the database

All the data for our application is stored on MariaDB. When a request is made for retrieving the list of available students, we run a query on our `course_registry` database. Running a single query at a time is simple but as the application gets popular, we will have more concurrent users. As the number of concurrent connections to the database increases, we will have to make sure that our database server is optimized to handle that load. In this section, we will look at the different types of caching that can be performed in the database. Let's start with query caching. Query caching is available by default on MariaDB; to verify if the installation has a query cache, we will use the `have_query_cache` global variable.

 Global variables are a type of system variables that affect the overall operation of the MariaDB server.

Let's use the SHOW VARIABLES command to verify if the query cache is available on our MariaDB installation, as shown in the following screenshot:

```
MariaDB [(none)]> show variables like 'have_query_cache';
+------------------+-------+
| Variable_name    | Value |
+------------------+-------+
| have_query_cache | YES   |
+------------------+-------+
1 row in set (0.00 sec)
```

Now that we have a query cache, let's verify if it is active. To do this, we will use the `query_cache_type` global variable, shown as follows:

```
MariaDB [(none)]> show variables like 'query_cache_type';
+------------------+-------+
| Variable_name    | Value |
+------------------+-------+
| query_cache_type | ON    |
+------------------+-------+
1 row in set (0.00 sec)
```

From this query, we can verify that the query cache is turned on. Now, let's take a look at the memory that is allocated for the query cache by using the `query_cache_size` command, shown as follows:

```
MariaDB [(none)]> show variables like 'query_cache_size';
+------------------+----------+
| Variable_name    | Value    |
+------------------+----------+
| query_cache_size | 67108864 |
+------------------+----------+
1 row in set (0.00 sec)
```

The query cache size is currently set to 64 MB; let's modify our query cache size to 128 MB.

> It is important to understand that the query cache is flushed on every query update. A really heavy system will benefit well with a bigger cache. Thorough testing will still be needed to determine the effects of the query cache.

The following screenshot shows the usage of the SET GLOBAL syntax:

```
MariaDB [course_registry]> set global query_cache_size=134217728;
Query OK, 0 rows affected (0.00 sec)

MariaDB [course_registry]> show variables like 'query_cache_size';
+------------------+-----------+
| Variable_name    | Value     |
+------------------+-----------+
| query_cache_size | 134217728 |
+------------------+-----------+
1 row in set (0.00 sec)
```

We use the SET GLOBAL syntax to set the value for the `query_cache_size` command, and we verify this by reloading the value of the `query_cache_size` command. Now that we have the query cache turned on and working, let's look at a few statistics that would give us an idea of how often the queries are being cached.

To retrieve this information, we will query the `Qcache` variable, as shown in the following screenshot:

```
MariaDB [course_registry]> SHOW STATUS LIKE 'Qcache%';
+-------------------------+-----------+
| Variable_name           | Value     |
+-------------------------+-----------+
| Qcache_free_blocks      | 1         |
| Qcache_free_memory      | 134208728 |
| Qcache_hits             | 44        |
| Qcache_inserts          | 1         |
| Qcache_lowmem_prunes    | 0         |
| Qcache_not_cached       | 77        |
| Qcache_queries_in_cache | 0         |
| Qcache_total_blocks     | 1         |
+-------------------------+-----------+
8 rows in set (0.00 sec)
```

From this output, we can verify whether we are retrieving a lot of statistics about the query cache. One thing to verify is the `Qcache_not_cached` variable that is high for our database. This is due to the use of prepared statements. The prepared statements are not cached by MariaDB. Another important variable to keep an eye on is the `Qcache_lowmem_prunes` variable that will give us an idea of the number of queries that were deleted due to low memory. This will indicate that the query cache size has to be increased.

From these stats, we understand that for as long as we use the prepared statements, our queries will not be cached on the database server. So, we should use a combination of prepared statements and raw SQL statements, depending on our use cases. Now that we understand a good bit about query caches, let's look at the other caches that MariaDB provides, such as the table open cache, the join cache, and the memory storage cache. The table open cache allows us to define the number of tables that can be left open by the server to allow faster look-ups. This will be very helpful where there is a huge number of requests for a table, and so the table need not be opened for every request. The join buffer cache is commonly used for queries that perform a full join, wherein there are no indexes to be used for finding rows for the next table. Normally, indexes help us avoid these problems. We will go over indexes in *Chapter 10*, *Performance Optimization*. The memory storage cache, previously known as the heap cache, is commonly is used for read-only caches of data from other tables or for temporary work areas.

Let's look at the variables that are with MariaDB, as shown in the following screenshot:

```
MariaDB [course_registry]> show variables like '%cache%';
+--------------------------------+------------+
| Variable_name                  | Value      |
+--------------------------------+------------+
| aria_pagecache_age_threshold   | 300        |
| aria_pagecache_buffer_size     | 134217728  |
| aria_pagecache_division_limit  | 100        |
| binlog_cache_size              | 32768      |
| binlog_stmt_cache_size         | 32768      |
| have_query_cache               | YES        |
| join_cache_level               | 2          |
| key_cache_age_threshold        | 300        |
| key_cache_block_size           | 1024       |
| key_cache_division_limit       | 100        |
| key_cache_segments             | 0          |
| max_binlog_cache_size          | 4294963200 |
| max_binlog_stmt_cache_size     | 4294963200 |
| metadata_locks_cache_size      | 1024       |
| query_cache_limit              | 131072     |
| query_cache_min_res_unit       | 4096       |
| query_cache_size               | 9999360    |
| query_cache_strip_comments     | OFF        |
| query_cache_type               | ON         |
| query_cache_wlock_invalidate   | OFF        |
| stored_program_cache           | 256        |
| table_definition_cache         | 400        |
| table_open_cache               | 400        |
| thread_cache_size              | 128        |
+--------------------------------+------------+
24 rows in set (0.00 sec)
```

Database caching is a very important step towards making our application scalable. However, it is important to understand when to cache, the correct caching techniques, and the size for each cache. Allocation of memory for caching has to be done very carefully as the application can run out of memory if too much space is allocated. A good method to allocate memory for caching is by running benchmarks to see how the queries perform, and have a list of popular queries that will run often so that we can begin by caching and optimizing the database for those queries. Now that we have a good understanding of database caching, let's proceed to application-level caching.

Caching in the application

Memory caching is another popular technique for making data available for quick retrieval. We will use memory caching to avoid roundtrips to the database servers. As the application grows, we will have to scale it out, and the calls from the web server to fetch data in the database server will get expensive. Memory caching can be used to avoid continuous roundtrips by storing data in the memory. Memory caching is commonly used to store the short-term volatile data, which helps in returning the data faster as it is stored in the memory. Memory caching should not be used as a solution to store persistent data, and it should only be used as a data store for volatile data. Let's dive into the world of memory caching using **memcached**.

Memcached is a fast, multithreaded, in-memory key-value store that we will use for storing serialized objects. These serialized objects will contain the output from our database calls, and they can also be used to store the output of an API call in the future. They can even store the output of our web pages after they are rendered and return the page output on subsequent requests, rather than building dynamic views on the server. To work with memcached, we will have to install the software and the required connection drivers to work with PHP. In this code snippet, we install memcached and PHP's driver for memcached:

```bash
#! /bin/bash

## installs memcached
sudo apt-get install -y memcached

## installs php's connection driver for memcached
sudo apt-get install -y php5-memcached

## restarts Apache web server
sudo service apache2 restart
```

Now that we have installed memcached, let's create our caching library to implement the set and get methods to add and retrieve data from memory, as shown in the following code snippet from lib/Cache.php:

```php
<?php

class Cache{
public $_cache;

public function __construct(){
```

```
                    $this->_cache = new Memcached();
                    $this->_cache->addServer('localhost',11211);
        }

public function set($key, $value, $expires=600){
return $this->_cache->set($key, $value, $expires);
        }

public function get($key){
return $this->_cache->get($key);
        }


}
```

In this snippet, we create our caching library. We begin by creating an object for `Memcached`, and then use the `addServer` method to connect to our local `memcache` server. Once we have the connection to memcache, we will pass the object to our `set` and `get` methods. The `set` method expects a unique key, a value that the unique key will carry, and the amount of time in seconds by which the data should be stored in the memory. The `get` method expects a key and retrieves the data for that key from the memory; if the key does not exist, it will return `false`. Now, let's make an object of this class available to the application. We will create an instance of this class in `Base_Controller` to make it available to our controllers, as shown in the following code from `controllers/Base_Controller.php`:

```
public function __construct(){
                $this->view = new Base_View();
                $this->logger = new Logger();
                $this->cache = new Cache();
                Session::init();
        }
```

In this snippet, we update the constructor of our `Base_Controller` class and add an instance of our caching library. Now that we have added the instance to the caching library available, let's add our student data to the cache and retrieve it from there, as shown in the following code snippet from `controllers/students.php`:

```
public function get($id=null){
                $this->logger->info("get action been requested");
                $this->view->message = $_GET['message'];

if(isset($_GET['message']) && $_GET['message']=='importSuccess'){
                        $this->view->message = 'Import is
                        successful';
```

```
                    }

                    $student_data = $this->cache->get('student_data');

if(!$student_data){

                            $student_data = $this->model-
                              >getStudents();
                            $this->cache->set('student_data',
                              $student_data);
                    }

                    $this->view->student_data = $student_data;
                    $this->view->render('students/get');
          }
```

In this snippet, we update the existing `get` method in the `student` controller to use our cache object to `store` and `retrieve` the contents from the memory. We can also use `memcache` to store sessions in the memory, which will allow a faster retrieval of user role and permissions list on a page load. To store the sessions on `memcache`, we will modify `session.save_handler` in our `php.ini` file, as shown in the following code from `/etc/php5/apache2/php.ini`:

```
session.save_handler = memcache
session.save_path = "127.0.0.1:11211"
```

In this snippet, we set the path to store the sessions on a local `memcache` instance; once the process of scaling out begins, this should be replaced by the host name or the IP address of the dedicated `memcache` cluster. Now that we have an idea of how `memcache` can be used for the purpose of memory caching, let's take a look at few other caches that can be used for caching purposes.

Advanced caching techniques

In the last two sections, we discussed database caching and memory caching to store data for faster retrieval. In this section, we will go over caches such as OpCache and Varnish. PHP is an interpreter language and the code has to be executed every single time. The process of execution happens in two steps, where the code is converted into operational byte code and is then executed. PHP 5.5 arrives with OpCache that caches the precompiled bytecode present in the memory and executes it. Though OpCache arrives by default with PHP 5.5, it is not enabled by default. To enable OpCache, we have to modify our `php.ini` file, as shown in the following code from `/etc/php5/apache2/php.ini`:

```
opcache.enable=1
opcache.memory_consumption=64
opcache.use_cwd=1
```

In this snippet, we enable OpCache and allocate 64 MB of memory for storing the bytecode. We also enable the `use_cwd` setting to append the current working directory to the script key. This will avoid any collisions between our cache keys. Once the changes are made, the web server has to be restarted for the changes to be applied. To verify the performance gains, we can use a profiler such as `xhprof` to understand how OpCache helps us by caching the bytecode.

The last type of caching will be page caching using Varnish. Varnish is a reverse proxy server that shields the web server from a massive traffic spike by storing the HTML pages in memory. Varnish has a few other competitors, but is considered to be very good at working as a reverse proxy. The installation and configuration of Varnish is beyond the scope of discussion here since building a reverse proxy in itself is a vast topic to cover.

Summary

In this chapter, we began by going over the basics of caching and why caching has to be implemented into an application. We discussed the different types of caching that are available and covered database caching with MariaDB, memory caching with Memcached, and bytecode caching with OpCache. In the next chapter, we will discuss the basics of the REST architectural design and build a REST API to allow external applications to interact with our student portal.

8
REST API

In the last chapter, we discussed different types of caching and implemented database caching, memory caching, and content caching. Our application currently allows users to view student and course information. An important thing to note here is that a user has to access the application to view the data. In this chapter, let's build an **Application Programming Interface (API)** that will allow another application to request for data from our application. An API is a collection of rules that describes how one application can interact with another application. In our case, we will build a REST API that will allow an external application to perform add and fetch operations.

What is REST?

Representational state transfer (REST) is an architectural design for designing communication and operational channels among networked applications. The REST design is commonly implemented while building web HTTP APIs. As REST APIs interact through HTTP requests, they provide heterogeneous interoperability. RESTful APIs are best used when a single web page has to show data from multiple partners. Let's take the example of a website that hosts movie reviews. There could be multiple sections powered by different partners on any review page on that site. These can be ad partners to display ads, third-party recommendation plugins to recommend similar movie reviews to the user, and social media plugins for comments, discussions, and to share the movie review with their friends. This is only possible due to smooth interaction between various services; implementing a RESTful API makes it more transparent.

In this section, let's begin by building a RESTful API that will allow an external application to access our application. A RESTful API can support the GET, POST, PUT, and DELETE HTTP methods. Before we proceed, let's take a look at the implementation of how we can translate different actions into URLs based on HTTP methods, as shown in the following table:

URL	Method	Description
api/students	GET	Fetches all the students
api/students	POST	Adds a student
api/students/1	PUT	Updates a student
api/students/1	DELETE	Deletes a student

The first thing to note is the similarity between the URL endpoints that we will use to perform the various actions. We use api/students to perform all the actions, but it has to be emphasized that the type of the HTTP method will determine the action that is performed for a request.

 We currently do not support the functionality to update and delete student information. This is a simple task that can be achieved by building actions to perform the activity.

Before we begin with building our API, we need to update our Bootstrap library; as the application grows, we have to move this functionality into a routing library and save it in the lib/Bootstrap.php file.

```
$ct_name = ucfirst($url[0]);

//for api
if($ct_name = "api"){
  $url[1] = $this->_routeApi();
}

$controller = new $ct_name;
```

We will add the preceding code to our Bootstrap library to check if the incoming request is for our API. If the incoming request is for the API, we will use the _routeApi method to determine the correct method that should handle this request.

Let's take a look at the processing of the incoming request in the _routeApi method using the following code snippet, present in the lib/Bootstrap.php file:

```php
private function _routeApi(){

    $method = $_SERVER['REQUEST_METHOD'];
    $action = "";

    switch($method){
        case "GET":
        $action = "get";
        break;
        case "POST":
        $action = "post";
        break;
        default:
        $action = "";
        break;
    }


    if(strlen($action)>0){
        return $action;
    }
    else{
        echo "Action is not available";
    }

}
```

In this snippet, we begin by retrieving the HTTP method for the incoming request from the $_SERVER super global. We will use the REQUEST_METHOD key to retrieve the HTTP method, and pass it into our switch block that would determine the correct action that should handle this request. Once the action is determined, we will return it. Now that we have implemented the routing for our API, let's build our API, present in the controllers/api.php file

```php
<?php

class Api extends Base_Controller{
    public $name;

    public function __construct(){
        $this->name = explode("/",$_REQUEST["url"])[1];
    }
}
```

In this snippet, we begin building our API by setting up our `Api` controller, and we retrieve the action for the current request. Now that we have the action, let's build the `get` and `post` methods to retrieve and add data using our API, as shown in the following code, present in the `controllers/api.php` file:

```php
public function get(){
  $method = "";
  $this->loadModel($this->name);

  switch($this->name){
    case "students":
    $method = "getStudents";
    break;
    case "courses":
    $method = "getCourses";
    break;
    default:
    break;
  }

  if(strlen($method)>0){
    $data = $this->model->$method();

    if(is_array($data) && count($data) >0){
      print _r($data);
    }
  }

}

public function post(){
  $method = "";
  $this->loadModel($this->name);

  switch($this->name){
    case "students":
    $method = "addStudent";
    break;
    case "courses":
    $method = "addCourse";
    break;
    default:
    break;
  }
```

```
  if(strlen($method)){
    $this->model->$method($_POST);
  }
}
```

In this snippet, we build our `get` and `post` methods, both of which begin by loading the required model based on the name of the controller that has been stored in the `$name` class variables. We will then pass in the name of the controller into a switch block that will determine the appropriate method. Based on the request, we will retrieve the data if it is a GET HTTP request, and add a student or a course if it is a POST HTTP request. In our `get` method, we fetch the required data and print it out on the page. In the next section, we will build a mechanism to generate an XML feed to send the data out as part of the response.

Generating XML feeds

In the last section, we built our API to fetch the data and print the raw data onto the page. In this section, we will build methods that will take the data and convert them into XML feeds. A remote application can then use these XML feeds to ingest the data. Before we build the XML generation functionality, let's create a class variable that can be used to hold this XML data using the following code in the `controllers/api.php` file:

```
public $xml;
```

Now that we have added the class variable, let's add the following XML generation functionality to our API, present in the `controllers/api.php` file:

```
private function _generateXML($root, $data){
  $this->xml = new SimpleXMLElement("<$root/>");

  foreach($data as $key=>$value){
    $this->_generateXMLChild(substr($root, 0, -1), $value);
  }
  header("HTTP/1.1 200 OK");
  header("Content-Type: application/xml; charset=utf-8");
  echo $this->xml->asXML();
}

private function _generateXMLChild($type ,$item){

  $child = $this->xml->addChild($type);
```

```
      foreach($item as $key => $value){
        $child->addChild($key, $value);
      }

    }
```

In this snippet, we create the `_generateXML` and `_generateXMLChild` methods to build the XML feed and print it. We use PHP's `SimplXMLElement` class to generate our XML feeds. In the `_generateXML` method, we expect two arguments: the name of the root element and the actual data. As the data that we will retrieve will be an array of arrays, we will have to loop over the parent array to retrieve the child arrays that carry the student data or course data. The child array is passed as an argument to the `_generateXMLChild`, which will be converted into XML. Once all the child arrays have been converted into XML, we will print this XML onto the page.

To use these methods to generate the XML feed, let's modify the `get` method using the following code, present in the `controllers/api.php` file:

```
  if(strlen($method)>0){
    $data = $this->model->$method();

    if(is_array($data) && count($data) >0){
      $this->_generateXML($this->name,$data);
    }
  }
```

In this snippet, we replaced the `print_r` call with a call to our `_generateXML` method. Now that we have generated an XML feed, let's work on generating a JSON feed.

Generating JSON feeds

In the last section, we used PHP's `SimplXMLElement` class to generate our XML feeds. In this section, we will use PHP's `json_encode` function to generate our JSON feed. Building a JSON feed is very simple when compared to building the XML feed. JSON is a very popular data exchange format and is considered lightweight when compared to XML, as shown in the following code snippet, present in the `controllers/api.php` file:

```
  private function _generateJSON($root, $data){
    header("HTTP/1.1 200 OK");
    header("Content-Type: application/json");
    echo json_encode(array($root=>$data));
  }
```

In this snippet, we begin by building our _generateJSON method that will expect the name of the endpoint and the data that was fetched by the get action. Now, let's modify the get action to use the _generateJSON method, as shown in the following code snippet:

```
if(strlen($method)>0){
  $data = $this->model->$method();

  if(is_array($data) && count($data) >0){
    $this->_generateJSON($this->name,$data);
  }
}
```

In this snippet, we replace the call to the _generateXML method with the _generateJSON method. Though we are replacing the XML feed with the JSON feed in this example, it is common to allow both feeds and let the external application decide which data format to choose. This is normally done by allowing an output format parameter in the query string, as shown in the following code:

```
api/students?output=json //generates JSON
api/students?output=xml //generates XML
```

Summary

In this chapter, we started by going over the concepts of REST architectural design. We moved forward by building a REST API that would support HTTP's GET and POST methods. Later, we built methods that would generate XML and JSON feeds to deliver content. In the next chapter, we will work on optimizing the security for our student portal. We will secure the application on all three fronts: Apache web server, PHP, and MariaDB database server.

9
Security

In the last chapter, we built a REST API that allows an external application to add and retrieve data to our database. In the earlier chapters, we built a whole application. However, before we make it accessible to the users, it is very important to go over the security of the total stack of software that the application is using. We have already introduced the concept of user authentication that partially helps with security in *Chapter 6, Authentication and Access Control*. In this chapter, we will primarily focus on tightening the security for our application.

This chapter will cover the following topics:

- Securing Apache web server
- Securing MariaDB
- Securing PHP

Securing the Apache web server

In this section, we will work on securing the Apache web server installation that our application is using. Apache web server is very widely used, and due to its popularity, there are numerous people who have figured out multiple ways to intrude into a non-secure Apache web server installation. A few issues that we will work on in this section are as follows:

- Hiding server information
- Server configuration limits

Let's begin by investigating the type of information leaks that occur while working with the Apache web server.

Hiding server information

A default installation of Apache web server provides a lot of information about the web server and the operating system that the server is installed on. Any information on the web server or the operating system can be used by mischievous users browsing the application to prepare for an attack on the web application. Exposing this information may help mischievous users prepare their attack on our web application. Let's begin by reviewing the information that the web server displayed to the user. We will test this by loading a page that does not exist and observe the response. The page appears as shown in the following screenshot:

One thing to observe from this screenshot is that we send the type and version of the web server. We also send the port and operating system information back via HTTP response. Now, let's make a few changes to our web server configuration files to avoid this. On the Ubuntu operating system that we use, these configurations are stored in the `security.conf` file. In other operating systems, these configurations are stored in the `apache2.conf` or `httpd.conf` files. Enter the following code snippet inside the `/etc/apache2/conf-available/security.conf` file:

```
ServerTokens Prod
ServerSignature Off
```

In the previous snippet, we modified the default values to server configuration directives. Here, we begin by modifying the value of `ServerTokens` from `Full` to `Prod`. `ServerTokens`, which is a directive that can be used to configure the data that is sent back from the web server as part of the response. `ServerSignature` is a server directive that is used to add an optional line containing the server and operating system information.

It is set to On by default, and we update it to Off. Now that we have updated the configurations, we will have to restart the web server using the following command:

```
service apache2 restart
```

In this snippet, we restart the web server to apply these directives. Now that we have applied these directives, let's go ahead and restart the web server again. Now, let's rerun the previous example to verify if the web server is still sending out the system information. The web page now appears as shown in the following screenshot:

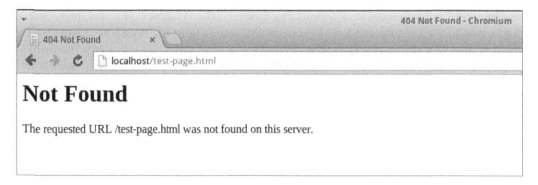

Upon reloading the page, we can confirm that the web server is not sending out the system information. Now, let's go ahead and set the server configuration limits to make sure that our application is not flooded by mischievous requests.

Server configuration limits

The Apache web server comes with predefined configurations, and we will go over a few of these configurations in this section. This section will help you understand these directives, and this knowledge can be used to fine-tune the web server according to our requirements. We add the following code snippet in the `/etc/apache2/conf-available/apache2.conf` file as per our requirements:

```
TimeOut 300
KeepAlive On
MaxKeepAliveRequests 100
KeepAliveTimeout 5
MaxClients 256
```

In the previous snippet, we looked at four very common Apache directives that help us. Here, the first directive that we will look at is the `Timeout` directive, which is used to set the amount of time the web server will wait to disconnect an open connection. This directive should be used carefully and cannot be generalized. However, 300 seconds is normally too long to keep a connection open; reducing the amount of time for timing out a connection should be considered. The next directive is the directive `KeepAlive`, which determines if persistent connections can be allowed. If `KeepAlive` is turned on, we can set the maximum number of requests to be allowed during a persistent connection using `MaxKeepAliveRequests`. The next directive that we will look at is `KeepAliveTimout`, which allows us to set the number of seconds to wait for the next request from the same client for the same connection. The last directive that we will look as is the `MaxClients` directive that sets the limit on the number of simultaneous requests that will be served by our Apache web server. The number of simultaneous requests should only be reached after thorough testing and application growth.

There are numerous web server directives that cannot be discussed at length. A few other recommendations to secure the web server are:

- Update the web server on a regular basis
- Set up `mod_security` and `mod_evasive` to build a firewall and network monitor
- Use name-based virtual hosting to avoid using direct IP addresses
- Regularly monitor access logs to understand and monitor the incoming traffic to make sure that there is no mischievous activity
- Now that we have looked at a few directives to secure our Apache web server installation, let's work on securing our MariaDB installation.

Securing MariaDB

In this section, we will cover a few topics that will help us secure our MariaDB database server. A few issues that we will cover in this section are:

- Password-protected access
- Building views to restrict access
- Creating users and granting access

Password-protected access

During the MariaDB installation process, the user is normally prompted to enter a password for the root user. It is not required to enter a password; users can hit escape to avoid entering a password. As we are trying to secure the installation, let's go over the steps to protect access by adding a password if the password was not added initially. We will use `mysqladmin` for this process and enter the following command:

```
mysqladmin -u root password <userpassword>
```

In this snippet, we set the new password of the `root` user. From here on, we will need this password to log in as the root user. Now that we have added the password to the root user, let's log in as the root user and go over the concepts of views.

Building views to restrict access

As our application grows, the number of tables that are needed to power the application grow too. To fetch data from multiple tables, we will have to perform certain joins that will make the query big. Views provide a way to hide this complexity by abstracting that complex query into a simpler query. Views are virtual tables, and they do not contain any data. Let's build a view in this section that would provide the data available in the `students`, `courses`, and `students_courses` tables, using the following command:

```
select s.student_id as student_id, c.course_id as course_id, s.first_
name, s.last_name, c.name, c.description
from students s
inner join students_courses sc on s.student_id=sc.student_id
inner join courses c on sc.course_id=c.course_id;
```

Now, let's build a view that will retrieve the data from this query available with a much simpler query. We will use the CREATE VIEW syntax for this view, as shown in the following command:

```
create view sc_view as
select s.student_id as student_id, c.course_id as course_id,
 s.first_name, s.last_name, c.name, c.description
from students s inner join
 students_courses sc on s.student_id=sc.student_id
inner join courses c on sc.course_id=c.course_id;
```

In this example, we build a view that will dynamically execute this query to generate the data. We use the CREATE VIEW command to create the view. Now that we have created the view, we can use the SELECT statement to query the view, as shown in the following command:

```
select * from sc_view;
```

This query will output the same data as the original query that was used to build this query. Similar to a table, views also have the ALTER and DROP DML statements. Now that we have added the view, a subset of our users will no longer need to view all the tables, they will only need access to the view. In the next section, we will create a user and grant them access only to the view.

Creating users and granting access

In this section, we will continue from the previous section to create a new user who will only have access to the sc_view table that was created. The MariaDB database server allows us to provide users with the access to the data they need. Let's begin by creating a read-only user in the MariaDB database by using the CREATE USER command:

```
create user 'ro_user'@'localhost' identified by 'password';
```

In this snippet, we create a user and provide a password for that user. The password for a user has to be more stringent when compared to the current password for this user. Now that we have our user, let's go ahead and provide access permissions to the view that we created in the last section by using the following command:

```
grant select on 'course_registry'.'sc_view' to 'ro_user'@'localhost';
```

We use the GRANT command to provide very specific access to our ro_user on the sc_view table. Let's verify if our GRANT command was successful by logging in to our MariaDB server by using the new credentials. The screenshot of the output is as follows:

```
root@adminuser-VirtualBox:/etc/apache2/conf-available# mysql -u ro_user -ppassword
Welcome to the MariaDB monitor.  Commands end with ; or \g.
Your MariaDB connection id is 45
Server version: 5.5.36-MariaDB-1~saucy-log mariadb.org binary distribution

Copyright (c) 2000, 2014, Oracle, Monty Program Ab and others.

Type 'help;' or '\h' for help. Type '\c' to clear the current input statement.

MariaDB [(none)]> use course_registry;
Reading table information for completion of table and column names
You can turn off this feature to get a quicker startup with -A

Database changed
MariaDB [course_registry]> show tables;
+---------------------------+
| Tables_in_course_registry |
+---------------------------+
| sc_view                   |
+---------------------------+
1 row in set (0.00 sec)
```

Now that we have logged in and verified that we only have access to sc_view, it will be a good effort to try to select the data from the view and try to drop the view to see if we will receive any errors while trying to drop the view. Working with user privileges can be a little tricky, and it is always recommended to use a tool such as phpMyAdmin to grant and revoke permissions. Use the following command to install phpMyAdmin:

```
sudo apt-get install -y phpmyadmin
```

Using this snippet, we install phpMyAdmin, and we can now start using it to perform day-to-day database activities, including controlling the privileges and permissions. Now that we have worked with the views and access permissions to secure our MariaDB server installation, let's work on securing our application by server-side filtering and XSS filtering.

Securing PHP

In this section, we will go over the possible security issues on the application side. It is always recommended to filter the content on the server. The filtering can be performed at various levels. We can begin by verifying if the type of the input that we expect is the same as the type of the input we get. We can use PHP's functions such as is_int, is_numeric, is_float, and is_string, explained as follows:

- is_int: This function is used to verify if the input is an integer
- is_numeric: This function is used to verify if the input is a number or a numeric string
- is_float: This function is used to verify if the input is a floating-point number
- is_string: This function is used to verify if the input is a string

Once we verify that the incoming input is same as expected, we can look for any cross-site scripting vulnerability that the incoming input may carry. To prevent any cross-site scripting vulnerability from creeping in, it is always advisable to filter the data before storing it in the database, and also escape the data while rendering it onto the page. We can use functions such as strip_tags, htmlspecialchars, and htmlentities to escape data from any script injections, explained as follows:

- strip_tags: This function is used to strip any HTML or PHP tag from a string (used for data sanitization)
- htmlspecialchars: This function is used to convert special characters into HTML entities (used for output escaping)
- htmlentities: This function is used to convert all applicable characters to HTML entities (used for output escaping)

While building applications, we should be very aware of SQL injections, and as we are using prepared statements, we need not worry about SQL injection attacks. For applications that don't use prepared statements, it is advisable to use the mysql_real_escape_string function provided by PHP. The final fix that we will make as part of this section is to hide the information that we are sending out as part of the response to the browser. The expose_php directive controls this and is located in the php.ini file, as shown in the following code:

```
; Decides whether PHP may expose the fact that it is installed on the
server
; (e.g. by adding its signature to the Web server header).  It is no
security
```

```
; threat in any way, but it makes it possible to determine whether you
use PHP; on your server or not.
; http://php.net/expose-php
expose_php = Off
```

By default, changing to Off will no longer expose the information about the PHP installation. As we are making a change to a PHP configuration, we will have to reload the web server.

Summary

In this chapter, we focused on securing our web server installation and the database server installation; we also discussed a few security fixes to handle various exploitation scenarios. This chapter is only intended to give us a basic platform to begin securing our application and the environment that we are hosting the application in. Security of an application is a journey rather than a destination, and it has to be revisited in frequent intervals. In the next chapter, we will discuss various performance optimization techniques to speed up our application.

10
Performance Optimization

In the last chapter, we went over different techniques to secure our web server installation and our database server; we also continued our work by adding filtering functionality that will help us sanitize the incoming data. In this chapter, we will go over a few techniques to optimize the performance of our software stack. Our application has already gained a performance increase due to the introduction of caching on various levels in *Chapter 7, Caching*. The aim of this chapter is to help us become aware of the options that are available for optimization, but not to implement these techniques from the get-go. Optimizing an application before thorough profiling may adversely affect the application. However, as developers, it is very important that we are aware of potential best-practice optimization techniques that are used while building our application. We will begin by discussing the optimizations that we will put in for our Apache web server and then we will go over MySQL query optimization and indexing. Finally, we will cover the different techniques to optimize our PHP code. We will be discussing the performance optimization techniques for the following topics:

- The Apache web server
- The MariaDB database server
- PHP

Performance optimization for the Apache web server

In this section, we will be going over the different steps to optimize our web server installation. Apache for a good part performs very well out-of-the-box but, as the application grows, we come across latencies or performance issues as the number of requests or transactions increases. A few issues that we will be addressing in this section are:

- Disabling unused modules
- Using compression
- Caching

Disabling unused modules

A default installation of the Apache web server arrives with a huge number of pre-installed modules. This is commonly very helpful for a variety of new projects when the main objective is to get hosted and be available to users quickly. A problem that we would notice as the application grows is the latency in responding to a request. A common cause of this problem is that the Apache modules are loaded into the memory and, if there are any modules that are unused, we can deactivate them and save memory. To get a list of the modules that are enabled, we can use Apache's command-line control interface. In the following snippet, we are using Apache's command-line control interface that has been built to help us understand and control the functioning of Apache daemon:

```
apache2ctl -M
```

This command will give us the results on a Debian/Ubuntu operating system. Another method to get a list of all the modules that have been is to use PHP's `apache_get_modules` function:

```php
<?php

echo '<h3>The List of Apache modules that are enabled.</h3>';

foreach(apache_get_modules() as $value){
        echo $value."<br />";
}

?>
```

In the preceding code snippet, we are using PHP's `apache_get_modules` function to print a list of modules that are enabled on Apache. This script has to be run in a browser and the script has to be hosted on Apache to retrieve this information. This script will not work if it is run via command line. The output of the script is shown in the following screenshot:

This output gives us a list of the modules that are currently enabled on our Apache web server. This list might be different based on the applications that we are running, and our application will not always require all the modules. As an example, we wouldn't need the `autoindex` module for our application, so let us disable this module using the `a2dismod` command.

When the `a2dismod` command is executed, it will remove the symlinks within `/etc/apache2/mods-enabled` that were generated by the `a2enmod` command when the module was enabled. For other operating systems than Ubuntu, the changes need to be made in the `httpd.conf` file. In the following snippet, we begin by disabling the `autoindex` module using the `a2dismod` command:

```
sudo a2dismod autoindex
sudo service apache2 restart
```

Now that we have disabled a module, we will have to restart the web server in order to notify about the current enabled modules. Disabling or enabling a module will always depend on the application at hand and has to be a well-informed decision performed after extensive testing. Now let us move onto the next optimization feature that will help us transfer compressed data across the wire, thereby helping us reduce the amount of the data that has to be transferred.

Using compression

It is always recommended to compress the content before responding to a request and thereby sending compressed content over the wire. The compressed data is uncompressed when the response reaches the browser, and once the response is uncompressed, the browser will render it. The best thing about this is that the end user will not be able to visibly tell that the response was compressed (unless they verify the HTTP headers). To compress the content on the server side, we will use the `deflate` module as shown in the following command. Currently this module is enabled but, if this module was disabled, we would use the `a2enmod` command to enable it:

```
sudo a2enmod deflate
sudo service apache2 restart
```

Another module that is recommended to use with compression is the `expires` module that helps us set the `Expires` HTTP header and `max-age` directive of the HTTP header that are part of the web server response. This will reduce the number of times a call is made to the webserver:

```
sudo a2enmod expires
sudo service apache2 restart
```

Similar to any other optimization techniques, both these modules have to be enabled on a production environment only after thorough testing on a test environment. It should be clearly documented in the tests if there were any unforeseen CPU spikes due to compression, and if the CPU spikes could adversely affect the performance of the web server. The last optimization technique that we will look at is a caching technique.

Caching

It is always recommended to implement caching in order to reduce the amount of overhead on the server. We can enable modules, such as the `disk_cache` module for disk caching and the `mem_cache` module for memory caching. It will again depend on the application that is being hosted and the amount of data that has to be cached will determine the caching method. Disk caching is preferred when there is a huge amount of data that has to be cached. It is always recommended to use external SSDs for disk caching purposes. If the amount of data that has to be cached is not very large, it can be cached in memory. As with any other optimization technique, it is recommended to thoroughly test this in a testing environment. A few other optimization techniques that need to be mentioned but that we will not be going deeply into are:

- The number of Apache processes and children should be limited
- The other background processes running on the same machine as the web server should be limited
- Piped logging should be the preferred logging method

Performance optimization for MariaDB

In this section, we will be going over the different steps for optimizing MariaDB. MariaDB already arrives with powerful algorithms that are used internally for performance optimization. Although the storage engines are optimized to run queries, we as developers should be aware of a few best practices that will help us build better queries. A few optimization techniques that we will be discussing in this section are:

- Best practices for data retrieval
- Understanding query execution
- Query optimization and indexes

Best practices for data retrieval

In a read-heavy environment, data retrieval will probably be the most common operation. Data retrieval, if not done correctly, can be a very processing-intensive process. It is always recommended to filter the data that is being retrieved in order to reduce the amount of processing that has to be done. The best practices that will be discussed more for data retrieval are as follows:

- It is recommended to avoid retrieving everything
- Use filters to retrieve what is required
- Limit the amount of data being retrieved
- Use query caching

Retrieving everything is not always good and it is not good while retrieving every record in a table. This is something that needs to be avoided, unless it is a very small table and the number of times the whole table is selected is very low. On the same line, it is always recommended to retrieve only the columns that are required and to avoid the use of SELECT * in a query. Even though it is required to retrieve all the columns, it is recommended to add all the required columns by the column name into the query and avoid the use of SELECT * in a query. Once we filter the number of columns that are required to retrieve a subset of the data, it is recommended to use the WHERE clause to filter the data that is being retrieved. Although we apply good filtering criteria, we might still have a lot of data, so it is recommended to use the LIMIT clause to only fetch a subset of the filtered data. Even though the paging is done on the application side, it is not recommended to retrieve all the records in the table to load them into the memory. It is recommended to use the LIMIT and OFFSET clauses to limit the amount of targeted data that needs to be retrieved. The last recommendation will be to always use query caching, so that the same query will not be executed multiple times. One thing to keep in mind is that MariaDB's query cache doesn't have a **Time To Live** feature (TTL) or time to expire feature and is flushed upon SQL updates. This can lead to data being cached for too long and delivering stale content; so, to avoid this, the RESET QUERY CACHE command has to be executed. Now that we know a few best practices for constructing queries, let's dive deeper to understand the process of query execution.

Understanding query execution

In this section, we will examine the flow in which the query is parsed and data is returned in a step-by-step manner. When a query is executed against a MariaDB server, it would first look to see if the data for this query has been cached in the query cache, if not, the query is passed onto the query parse. The query parser takes the query and builds a parse tree by dividing the query into segments. The parse tree generated by the query parser is then run through the syntactical checks to verify that the query is syntactically correct. Upon successful syntactical check of the query, it is passed to the query preprocessor, which in turn verifies the details such as whether the table and columns in the query exist and other finer details if the user executing the query has enough privileges to access the table. The query passes through the preprocessor; it is then sent to the query optimizer where the parse tree is converted into a query plan. A query can be executed in multiple ways to produce the exact same output and the query optimizer decides what is the best query plan to execute the current query in the least amount of time. We will go over query optimization and understand the different steps for the query optimizer in the next section. Once a query plan is selected from the query optimizer, it is passed to the query execution engine, which executes the query plan to perform the intended action.

Query optimization and indexing

In this section, we will begin by understanding the different operations performed by the query optimizer and understand how query optimization can be done. Later, we will work with a basic example of creating an index. A few of the different operations that the query optimizer is responsible for are:

- Coming up with the best order for the tables to be joined to make the query execution as easy as possible
- Applying the required algorithms to optimize the usage of any aggregate and mathematical rules in the query
- Optimizing the sort operations to use the least amount of resources
- Applying a short circuit for the filter conditions, as in; if the condition is bound to be false, then the whole query needs to be executed
- Optimizing the use indexes that are available

Now that we understand the process of the query optimization performed by the MariaDB server query optimizer, let us look at a few steps that we can take to understand and optimize our queries. Before we dive deep into optimization, let us pick a sample query for optimizing. We will use the `students` table and retrieve all the students whose first name starts with the letter "J". The output is shown in the following screenshot:

```
MariaDB [course_registry]> select student_id, first_name, last_name from students where first_name like 'J%' limit 5;
+------------+------------+-----------+
| student_id | first_name | last_name |
+------------+------------+-----------+
|          1 | John       | Doe       |
|          2 | Jane       | Dane      |
|          6 | James      | Price     |
|          7 | Jason      | Chau      |
|          8 | Joe        | North     |
+------------+------------+-----------+
5 rows in set (0.00 sec)
```

In this example, we are using a simple query to pull out the student ID, first name, and last name of students whose names begin with the letter "J". As part of our best practices, we are only retrieving the top five records. Now to get a deeper understanding about our query, let us use the EXPLAIN keyword. The output is shown in the following screenshot:

```
MariaDB [course_registry]> explain select student_id, first_name, last_name from students where first_name like 'J%' limit 5;
+----+-------------+----------+------+---------------+------+---------+------+------+-------------+
| id | select_type | table    | type | possible_keys | key  | key_len | ref  | rows | Extra       |
+----+-------------+----------+------+---------------+------+---------+------+------+-------------+
|  1 | SIMPLE      | students | ALL  | NULL          | NULL | NULL    | NULL |   13 | Using where |
+----+-------------+----------+------+---------------+------+---------+------+------+-------------+
1 row in set (0.00 sec)
```

Upon executing the previous query (the EXPLAIN keyword), we get to notice a few things that point out that our query is not optimized. A point to understand is that, even though we are using a WHERE clause to filter the data, the engine still has to read all the rows in the table to retrieve this information. This is called a table scan, and table scans should be avoided to extract the best performance. The best way to avoid a table scan is by having an index on the column that is being used for the filtering purposes. Let us go ahead and create an index to help us optimize our query. In the following command snippet, we are using the ALTER TABLE DDL command to add an index on the first name column in the table:

```
alter table students add key IX_first_name(first_name);
```

Upon creating an index, let us rerun our previous query with the EXPLAIN keyword to see if the index is helping us optimize our query. The output is shown in the following screenshot:

Upon running the previous query after adding an index, we can notice that our query is no longer performing a table scan but is using the index to pick the students whose first name begins with the letter "J". Indexing by itself is a very important concept that has to be dealt with very carefully, so it is always recommended to test intensively before building indexes in a production environment. It is important to keep in mind that indexes can sometimes also slow down the application. Let us consider the case of a write-heavy environment, for every write to the database, there will have to be an update to the index. Therefore, it is important to understand that an index should not be built for every column and should only be built for columns that will be used for operations such as filtering, aggregating, and sorting. A good practice is to monitor the slow queries using the slow query log and begin by optimizing those slow queries. As working with the slow query login itself is a very big topic, it is beyond the scope of this book to discuss it further. In the next section, let us look at a few best practices to optimize the performance for our PHP code.

Performance optimization for PHP

Now that we have discussed a good number of optimization techniques for our Apache web server and MariaDB, let us look at a few best practices that will help us optimize the performance of our PHP code. In this section, the best practices that we will go over are as follows:

- Closing any open resource connections
- Reducing the number of calls to the database
- Encouraging the use of JSON data format for data exchange.

It is always recommended to close out any open resource connections such as database connections or file handles. The resources can get intensive on the machine as the number of the requests for database connections and file handles increase. Therefore, it is not a good idea to keep any of these connections open. The next technique to help us optimize performance would be to reduce the number of calls to the database, mainly if the database is not on the same machine as the web server. Network resources and bandwidth have to be factored into this decision, as the fewer the calls to the database, the less the use of network resources. The last optimization recommendation would be application-specific, where it is encouraged to use JSON data format for delivering data. XML, another popular data format, is very heavy when compared to the JSON, and encouraging the JSON data format for exchange will help us save the amount of data that is being transferred across the wire. These are a few performance optimization recommendations for our PHP code. In the next section, we will be dealing with very advanced performance enhancement techniques such as using content delivery networks, reverse proxies for static caching, and database replication in the master-slave database architecture.

CDN, reverse proxy, and database replication

In this section, we will be briefly introduced to **Content Delivery Network (CDN)**, reverse proxies, and the concept of database replication. Use of either or all of CDN, reverse proxies, or database replication is necessary when the application grows and receives a huge number of requests per second. A CDN is a huge set of servers that are deployed across multiple geographical locations. The purpose of a CDN is to deliver content to the end user from the nearest possible server. As an example, a website hosted in the US gets a request from a user in India. For this request to be complete, it will take a fair amount of time for the server in the US to process the response and send it over to the user in India. It would be easier if the content was housed close-by, so that the amount of time taken to complete the request will be shorter. CDNs help us solve this problem, where they would store static content on their servers and serve that content to the end user from the nearest available server. Reverse proxies are similar to CDNs where they store and deliver static content, but they are not necessarily available closer to the end user. Reverse proxies that are popularly used are Varnish and Squid. The final topic that we will go over for this chapter is the concept of database replication. As the application grows, it is very hard for a single database server to handle all the incoming requests. It is very common for a single master database server to be supported by extra slave nodes that share the incoming requests. Database replication is used to keep the slave database servers up-to-date with the master database server.

Summary

In this chapter, we have discussed the different optimization techniques and best practice methods to work with Apache, MariaDB, and PHP. Performance optimization is a very important concept but is probably not needed for many websites from the get-go. However, it is always necessary to keep an eye open and be ready to optimize the system when required. Application downtime and page load time are very important for the successful working and progress of a website, and performance optimization will help avoid application downtime and fasten the page load.

We have covered a variety of topics beginning with the basics of MariaDB and programming with PHP to advanced topics such as caching, security, and performance optimization. Web application development is a journey and not a destination, and this book will help us lay a strong foundation for building a robust web application.

Index

Thank you for buying
Building a Web Application with PHP and MariaDB: A Reference Guide

About Packt Publishing

Packt, pronounced 'packed', published its first book "*Mastering phpMyAdmin for Effective MySQL Management*" in April 2004 and subsequently continued to specialize in publishing highly focused books on specific technologies and solutions.

Our books and publications share the experiences of your fellow IT professionals in adapting and customizing today's systems, applications, and frameworks. Our solution based books give you the knowledge and power to customize the software and technologies you're using to get the job done. Packt books are more specific and less general than the IT books you have seen in the past. Our unique business model allows us to bring you more focused information, giving you more of what you need to know, and less of what you don't.

Packt is a modern, yet unique publishing company, which focuses on producing quality, cutting-edge books for communities of developers, administrators, and newbies alike. For more information, please visit our website: www.packtpub.com.

About Packt Open Source

In 2010, Packt launched two new brands, Packt Open Source and Packt Enterprise, in order to continue its focus on specialization. This book is part of the Packt Open Source brand, home to books published on software built around Open Source licenses, and offering information to anybody from advanced developers to budding web designers. The Open Source brand also runs Packt's Open Source Royalty Scheme, by which Packt gives a royalty to each Open Source project about whose software a book is sold.

Writing for Packt

We welcome all inquiries from people who are interested in authoring. Book proposals should be sent to author@packtpub.com. If your book idea is still at an early stage and you would like to discuss it first before writing a formal book proposal, contact us; one of our commissioning editors will get in touch with you.

We're not just looking for published authors; if you have strong technical skills but no writing experience, our experienced editors can help you develop a writing career, or simply get some additional reward for your expertise.

Learning FuelPHP for Effective PHP Development

ISBN: 978-1-78216-036-6 Paperback: 104 pages

Use the flexible FuelPHP framework to quickly and effectively create PHP applications

1. Scaffold with oil - the FuelPHP command-line tool.

2. Build an administration quickly and effectively.

3. Create your own project using FuelPHP.

Persistence in PHP with Doctrine ORM

ISBN: 978-1-78216-410-4 Paperback: 114 pages

Build a model layer of your PHP applications successfully, using Doctrine ORM

1. Develop a fully functional Doctrine-backed web application.

2. Demonstrate aspects of Doctrine using code samples.

3. Generate a database schema from your PHP classes.

Please check **www.PacktPub.com** for information on our titles

Getting Started with MariaDB

ISBN: 978-1-78216-809-6   Paperback: 100 pages

Learn how to use MariaDB to store your data easily and hassle-free

1. A step-by-step guide for installing and configuring MariaDB.

2. Includes real-world examples that help you learn how to store and maintain data on MariaDB.

3. Written by someone who has been involved with the project since its inception.

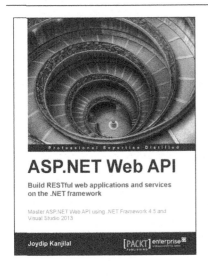

ASP.NET Web API
Build RESTful web applications and services on the .NET framework

ISBN: 978-1-84968-974-8   Paperback: 224 pages

Master ASP.NET Web API using .NET Framework 4.5 and Visual Studio 2013

1. Clear and concise guide to the ASP.NET Web API with plentiful code examples.

2. Learn about the advanced concepts of the WCF-windows communication foundation.

3. Explore ways to consume Web API services using ASP.NET, ASP.NET MVC, WPF, and Silverlight clients.

Please check **www.PacktPub.com** for information on our titles

Made in the USA
Monee, IL
30 June 2021